MW00777253

Forced Out

THE GEORGE AND SAKAYE ARATANI NIKKEI IN THE AMERICAS SERIES

Series Editors LANE HIRABAYASHI, VALERIE MATSUMOTO, AND TRITIA TOYOTA

This series endeavors to capture the best scholarship available illustrating the evolving nature of contemporary Japanese American culture and community. By stretching the boundaries of the field to the limit (whether at a substantive, theoretical, or comparative level), these books aspire to influence future scholarship in this area specifically and Asian American studies more generally.

Forced Out

Out

A Nikkei Woman's Search
for a Home in America

JUDY Y. KAWAMOTO

UNIVERSITY PRESS OF COLORADO
Louisville

Published by University Press of Colorado
245 Century Circle, Suite 202
Louisville, Colorado 80027

All rights reserved
Manufactured in the United States of America

 The University Press of Colorado is a proud member of
the Association of University Presses.

The University Press of Colorado is a cooperative publishing enterprise supported, in part, by Adams State University, Colorado State University, Fort Lewis College, Metropolitan State University of Denver, Regis University, University of Colorado, University of Northern Colorado, University of Wyoming, Utah State University, and Western Colorado University.

∞ This paper meets the requirements of the ANSI/NISO Z39.48–1992 (Permanence of Paper).

ISBN: 978-1-64642-070-4 (cloth)
ISBN: 978-1-64642-071-1 (ebook)
DOI: https://doi.org/10.5876/9781646420711

Library of Congress Cataloging-in-Publication Data

Names: Kawamoto, Judy, author. | Hirabayashi, Lane Ryo, writer of afterword.
Title: Forced out : a Nikkei woman's search for a home in America / Judy Y. Kawamoto.
Other titles: George and Sakaye Aratani Nikkei in the Americas series.
Description: Louisville : University Press of Colorado, [2020] | Series: The George and Sakaye Aratani Nikkei in the Americas series | Includes bibliographical references and index.
Identifiers: LCCN 2020029268 (print) | LCCN 2020029269 (ebook) | ISBN 9781646420704 (cloth) | ISBN 9781646420711 (ebook)
Subjects: LCSH: Kawamoto, Judy. | Japanese Americans—Biography. | Japanese American women—Biography. | Japanese Americans—Evacuation and relocation, 1942-1945. | World War, 1939-1945—Personal narratives, Japanese American. | Japanese Americans—Social conditions—20th century. | Psychotherapists—United States—Biography. | Social workers—United States—Biography. | LCGFT: Autobiographies.
Classification: LCC D769.8.A6 K38 2020 (print) | LCC D769.8.A6 (ebook) | DDC 940.53/145092 [B]—dc23
LC record available at https://lccn.loc.gov/2020029268
LC ebook record available at https://lccn.loc.gov/2020029269

This publication was made possible, in part, with support from the University of California Los Angeles's Aratani Endowed Chair in Asian American Studies.

For my parents, Rose and George Kawamoto.

At a time when everything was taken from them, they never let go of their humanity.

CONTENTS

PREFACE

Digging up stories about the past, about one's family, and about one's early life, wherever that may have taken place, can be a trying affair. So many of those stories, at least for me, have been difficult memories, memories of racism and hardship and poverty. Memories that under normal circumstances, one tries not to dwell on. In fact, growing up, my personal motto was not *try to remember* but *try to forget*.

But life doesn't always let you have your way.

There is a particular question I know I will be asked whenever I meet another Japanese American over the age of, say, fifty. A question I always have to respond to with the same disappointing answer.

The question: What camp was your family in?

My answer: We didn't go to a camp.

The questioner is not referring to Girl Scout camp or church camp or junior high school leadership camp. No, the questioner, clearly seeing I am a woman of Japanese ancestry, is referring to the World War II incarceration camps for Japanese Americans.

I say that my answer is disappointing because upon hearing that I don't have a camp story to share, the questioner usually soon loses interest in talking with me, probably because he or she feels like there isn't much to talk about with this stranger who doesn't, after all, have any shared history.

Over time I found myself dreading this question and hating to have to give my same, off-putting answer. After awhile, I found that this repeated ritual left me feeling frustrated and, yes, a little irritated. But worst of all, it left me feeling unseen and like a perpetual outsider, a feeling so familiar to me from growing up when and where I did. I finally decided it was time to do something about this ritual, these distasteful feelings. It was time to tell my family's story.

I am completely aware that the forced removal and incarceration of all Japanese American people from the West Coast of the United States was the defining event of their lives and had a plethora of tangible and intangible psychological ramifications for the generations that followed, even up to the present time. Two-thirds of these innocent victims were American citizens by birth; the other third were their elders, immigrant parents, and grandparents. My family shared in that destructive, defining experience, which, I would argue, left its indelible markings on my life and the lives of my siblings.

But as I have had to explain so often, my parents never went to a camp. They were forced from their home in Seattle with the 120,000 others along the entire West Coast, but they had the good fortune to be able to avoid an incarceration camp. The War Relocation Authority, part of the military, granted Dad permission to take his family—at that time consisting of Mom and my sister Lilian—to live in Wyoming, a state outside the "security area." There they would join Dad's parents, who were modestly successful vegetable gardeners in Sheridan and up till then had been considered upstanding members of the community. After all, Grandpa was a member of the Rotary Club, though that was soon to change; his membership would be rescinded in the racist war hysteria that followed.

This part of the American story, of the few exiles scattered willy-nilly across the country, seems virtually unknown even to a surprising number of Japanese Americans, let alone to that portion of the general public who knows anything at all about the forced removal and incarceration of Japanese Americans. Over the years I've made random searches in books and journals to see if I could find any statistics on this group, and I've usually come up empty-handed. It was only very recently that, searching the internet, I found figures for how many Japanese Americans were evacuated but not incarcerated. I was very surprised to at last find some information and more surprised yet to see that the total number was just under 5,000 people, more than I had expected. Nearly all had gone to states adjacent to the West Coast, but a few went to inland parts of Washington and Oregon as well as to the plains state of Illinois. There were over 300 persons removed for whom no states were named.

Throughout the essays in this volume, I have made reference to various aspects of the period after Pearl Harbor and the removal of Japanese Americans. I have referenced Executive Order 9066, the forced removal, the incarceration, and my parents' exile from Seattle. I have used these references merely to give basic context to the essays themselves. It is not my intention to give a general history of the forced removal and incarceration of all Japanese Americans. For that, the reader can turn to any number of excellent references now available on the subject.

I have tried not to be too repetitive but also have not wanted to place unfair assumptions on the reader. Even if you encounter either or both of these failings, I hope you will hang in there anyway, keep reading, and become familiar with a family in a doubly unusual circumstance.

My goals in writing these stories are to bring light to this unknown aspect of a sliver of disgraceful American history and to disprove the myth that managing to avoid the camps meant that we got off easy and our lives could proceed as normal.

Most of all, these stories are meant to be a tribute to my parents and how they handled their lives with dignity, honesty, and perseverance after losing their home and all their earthly possessions when they were forced to leave Seattle. That in itself is not what, for me, made it so important to tell their story, to make it part of the public record. After all, in losing their homes, businesses, and personal belongings, they were not unlike the rest of the Japanese Americans on the West Coast. But that is where the similarity ends, where my parents' story is different from the stories of the vast majority of those who were forcibly removed. While their friends, everyone they knew, and everyone else in general spent the next two to three years imprisoned in American concentration camps—"internment camps" was the name that was commonly used—located around the United States, my parents went off to Wyoming by themselves. This may not seem like such a big difference, but it was huge. Yes, it spared my family from the camp experience, but it also cut them off from their community—from any community that looked like them, shared a language that wasn't English, ate the same food, automatically held similar beliefs about how to treat and interact with each other. People who could give them a sense of belonging and a shared understanding that they were all in this together and that together they would make it through. With only my grandparents to turn to, they were on their own, isolated, shaped by their need to survive in a perversely hostile world.

These stories are told through my eyes and from my perspective. They include factual information about my family, primarily during the time directly after they were forced from Seattle, when we were living on our farm in Montana, and, later, during our transition to life in Denver. I can be specific about that struggle only for myself, telling the details of only my personal response, starting with suddenly being faced with a large, all-white junior high school in a large, all-white city. The time I became consciously aware of the lack of a likeness in anyone around me. I can speak for my siblings in describing the general experience of such a life-changing move with the knowledge that their lives were as deeply affected as mine in those tangible and intangible social and psychological ways. The specific details of their experiences remain theirs to tell should they choose to do so.

You will also find stories here that include my adult experiences: as a young idealist in Philadelphia, as a psychotherapist in the Bay area, and on trips to New York City, Cape Town, and London—all mixed together with stories of growing up in Montana on an isolated farm near an Indian reservation. I include them because no matter where I was, my childhood was always with me, forcing me to look at that bigger world beyond to find the ways I or my family was reflected back. Ironically, I now realize that in this way, my experience has not been so different from that of my parents after their removal from Seattle.

So while these stories are my own, about my life, they are also a way of telling about my parents and their lives, their struggles to live, love, grieve, and persist. Taken together, they show that while things seem to change over time and with each generation, if one listens closely, one can always hear the echoes of the past.

Forced Out

PROLOGUE

In writing my family's story—my story—I have tried to be true to the facts as I have remembered them or been able to ascertain them from other people, photos, and research into the history of the time. My parents' and sister's lives in Seattle before Pearl Harbor and their forced removal to Wyoming are particularly hard to write about since everyone from that period is gone: my parents, my grandparents, and the historian of my generation, my older sister. The list leaves me heavy-hearted. I was not yet born when they were removed from Seattle, and over the course of growing up I remember hearing only snatches of conversations that referred to that time and that gave only hints as to what their lives were like.

Looking at the few photos of Mom, Dad, and Lilian from her birth till around age three, I am captivated. Some of the photos are large, professionally taken, and sepia in tone; others are small, on shiny photo paper with a generous band of white, sometimes with ruffled edging around them. None are in color. What I see in the way they are dressed, the way they look into the camera, and especially the expressions on their faces reassures me that this was a happy time, a time of contentment and promise.

They, my parents, were so young when they married. My mother was only eighteen and my father just five years her senior. I can't imagine being married at eighteen. When I was that age I knew nothing about anything, least of all about a serious relationship, a relationship important enough to end in marriage. I am guessing that my mother didn't really know much either. Their marriage was arranged, which was not unusual for their day or our culture. I heard later in my adulthood that had either of them protested vociferously, the marriage would not have taken place. But Mom was so young and naive, I doubt she could have even discerned whether she had anything to protest. I don't know whether Dad knew any more than Mom when it came to serious relationships. And that is a big, sad, gaping hole for me and my remaining siblings: what we know about either of our parents before they met and married could probably be written on a slip of paper the size of the fortune in a fortune cookie.

A short time ago, in an attempt to see if I could find out anything more or more substantial about my parents' lives, I decided to visit Seattle, walk the old neighborhood where they had lived, get a feel for the city they were making their own before Executive Order 9066 sent them packing to the countryside. My sister Mary sent me copies of several documents from old files of our parents that gave me an idea where to look, what neighborhood to walk. It was no surprise to find that they had lived in what is called the International District. In their day, that neighborhood was mostly taken up by the city's Chinatown and Japantown; today, it also includes Seattle's Koreatown as well as concentrations of other Asian ethnic groups like Cambodians, Laotians, and Vietnamese. It is not a large area but also not small, given its diversity of inhabitants, and it's located in the center of Seattle, a short walk to the water. Like much of the rest of Seattle, it has its share of hills but is not too steep to keep foot traffic from being heavy—even the elders can be seen walking to and from their shopping destinations. I felt smug about the fact that, coming from Berkeley and the San Francisco area, I was used to hills and could navigate on foot pretty comfortably.

An old Berkeley friend, Loren, now living in Oregon offered to meet me in Seattle and help me explore some of the places I wanted to contact. My plan was to visit landmarks in the International District and look specifically for the addresses my parents had any connection to. The only other place I was determined to visit was the University of Washington. I would find that a little hand-holding on this emotional journey turned out to be much appreciated. I had been enthusiastic about stepping through this narrow opening into my parents' and sister's past, but it was a bittersweet experience. I knew it would be painful, and there were moments when I felt the pain acutely.

Shortly before I left for Seattle, someone passed along to me a paperback titled *The Hotel on the Corner of Bitter and Sweet* by Jamie Ford. The timing was right because if I'd waited until after my trip to read it, I might have completely missed the Panama Hotel, the hotel of the novel's title.

The Panama is a landmark in the International District not only because of its importance as a business establishment but also because when word of the exclusion came down, many of the Japanese American residents in the area were allowed to store some of their belongings in the hotel basement. After the war, many of these residents were unable to reclaim their trunks and suitcases and boxes, which were left in the hotel basement to gather dust. Years later, they were discovered. Much to the credit of the current owner, she fully grasped what she had acquired, saved the baggage, and made a small historical museum out of the hotel and the abandoned pieces. I hadn't been successful in arranging an appointment to visit the basement, so when Loren and I made it to the Panama, the owner was not there. As much as we wanted to, we weren't able to go down to the bowels of the building and view the shelves and piles of abandoned boxes and trunks and suitcases, the personal belongings of people who had hoped to hold on to something of their lives by leaving them in that basement to be retrieved when the situation allowed.

The hotel is still in use. Completely renovated, it retains from its heyday in the first half of the twentieth century not only the overall structure but also some of the internal details like parts of the original wooden floors, the radiators, a few pieces of period furniture. What couldn't be saved or repaired was replaced or redone in the original style. I was given a tour of the upstairs, a peek inside the rooms, modest but clean and neat.

Seeing this historic building, knowing its role in the forced removal of the International District, knowing what still remained dusty and unclaimed in its basement all heightened for me the sadness, the feelings of loss and of lives interrupted, and the stark realization that while buildings can be renovated to look as they did in the past, lives are changed forever.

After the tour, Loren and I had a cup of tea in the lobby, now a tea room. We wanted to relax and quietly take in the atmosphere and the experience. Loren seemed to be enjoying herself, but for me it felt a little strange, slightly disrespectful, to be enjoying a quiet cup of tea above all that abandoned baggage. To be honest, it felt a little spooky. If I let myself, I could picture as well as feel the ghostly spirits of the owners, young men and women quietly rummaging through the baggage, finding the objects belonging to them, impatiently waiting to be released, waiting to return home. I couldn't imagine spending a night at the hotel. That basement was a far too busy place for my comfort.

Though the initial purpose of the trip was to connect with my own family's story, I also found myself pondering a much bigger picture: the meaning of the various levels of loss suffered by the city. The Japantown, the Nihonmachi, of pre-World War II Seattle was a thriving commercial and residential area, small but populated by successful businesses and professionals and their families. The sudden, overnight forced removal of an entire group of people en masse must have left the International District looking like a town intact but mysteriously empty. However, that look didn't last long; it is well documented that many whites quickly moved into the district and took over the empty businesses and other establishments left behind by the Nikkei. This would have been easy to do, since the buildings and businesses had been abandoned in such haste that everything was basically still the same and ready to be reopened for business as usual. I have also read that some of those taken-over establishments didn't survive, since those who were left in the area seemed in no hurry to patronize them.

As I wandered around the International District, I was always aware that the place I was seeing, smelling, hearing was completely different from the place where my parents and sister had lived for so many years before the war. The district never fully recovered from the loss of its Japanese American citizens. The city as a whole did not recover the totality of its lost population. The estimate is that about 65 percent to 70 percent of the incarcerated returned to Seattle. The Nihonmachi was virtually destroyed. Some research shows that not even half of the business establishments returned to the International District after the war. The financial loss to the city as a whole must have been tremendous: monetary loss to the Nikkei alone is calculated to have been in the many millions by today's standards.

The University of Washington (UW) also must have suffered quite an economic blow since practically overnight it lost 449 tuition-paying students—to say nothing of what the campus must have looked and felt like with so many students suddenly gone missing. For the remaining student population, it must have felt like a ghost town, perhaps with some of the ghosts still hovering about. Friends torn from friends, students from their teachers and mentors and the supportive guidance of the academic community. The university president, Lee Paul Sieg, is reported to have made a strong stand against the student removal, but he was no match for the federal government, the War Relocation Authority, and the hysterical racism of the moment. At least he has gone down in UW history as having taken the moral high ground.

After the war, though the Japanese Americans released from the camps were told they could return to their homes, for most there were no "homes" to return to. So many homes and businesses had been commandeered by whites. In Seattle as in many urban areas along the West Coast, there were heated debates and strong feelings about accepting the returnees back into their cities and former communities. Eventually, the mayors and governors of Washington and California agreed to take back their former citizens, but the returnees were often greeted with taunts, name calling, and other behaviors that left no doubt in the minds of the Nikkei that they were still regarded as "the enemy" and that the road ahead for them would be anything but easy, pleasant, or friendly.

There are numerous and diverse stories as to why folks didn't return to the places they'd come from, and the majority of them are not happy ones. For our family, it was because the exclusion had forced us to become farmers, and farmers don't have the liberty to wake up one morning and decide to leave the farm that day or the next and do something else. Dad and Mom were pretty much stuck on the farm, working hard to make it pay off.

Reading about how the returning Nikkei were "greeted," hearing about their struggles to resettle against odds that appeared insurmountable, I finally had to grudgingly acknowledge that the Japanese American men who had volunteered for the United States Army and formed the now famous 442nd Regimental Combat Team turned out to be right: their unflagging, heroic service in the army not only proved their loyalty but also bolstered the message that all Japanese Americans were, in fact, loyal *American* citizens and had no loyalties to the enemy nation of Japan. The men, many of whom volunteered directly from the camps, consistently said that only volunteer military service would prove that Japanese Americans were not enemy spies, were not harboring a secret devotion to Japan, were not secretly collaborating with the enemy, and so forth. In fact, no case of spying or espionage for Japan by any Japanese American was ever discovered or reported. Ever.

I have learned over time that there is something about war that speaks in deafening tones to Americans of all ilk. All voices, pro or con, about any given war or "military conflict" can be made to become one when it comes to recognizing and honoring those lost to the slaughter of war. The recognition of the service of the 442nd, which became known as the regiment with the most fatalities of World War II, helped immensely in resettling the Nikkei. In big cities like Seattle, San Francisco, and Los Angeles, as well as in smaller cities and rural areas, white Americans were able to welcome back their fellow citizens with hearts more open and grateful because of the service and sacrifice of people once labeled as "the enemy."

As for me, I confess it has taken me many years to truly digest the fact that a man could volunteer to serve in the army of the country that had imprisoned him and his family in the concentration camp where they were all living at that time. I can only understand it as the supreme act of generosity and self-sacrifice and willpower.

Because I wanted to see the International District's present-day Asian American community as well, we visited two community organizations that document the area's history and offer services to residents. At the Japanese Community and Cultural Center of Washington, we encountered testaments to the past, including pictures of the immigrant generation and some of the business establishments that had existed prior to the exclusion and several iconic pictures of the exclusion: the displaced at a train station guarded by military men holding rifles with bayonets; families, some smiling self-consciously as if for the camera, some looking shell-shocked; the now well-known picture of a mother holding her child who was only slightly older than an infant. She wears a stylish hat and a nice coat, but her visage is unsmiling, her mouth turned down at the corners as if she knows that what lies ahead for her child is not at all what she had planned or imagined. Though most of these artifacts were familiar to me, they felt different, more grave and weighty, more frightening, here in the city where they actually happened.

Completely new to me were pictures about the importance of baseball in the Japanese American community before, during, and for some years after the war. Pre-war there had been a healthy, competitive exchange between teams from Japan and from the Seattle area, and surprisingly, this exchange resumed for some years following the war. I had heard and read that during their imprisonment in the camps, young men formed teams and played serious baseball within camp confines and that at some point, several teams were allowed to travel among camps to compete. But the fact that they had kept that joy of the sport alive between the two countries even after the war was news to me. I am anything but an enthusiastic sports fan, but baseball is one sport I enjoy watching and I feel lucky to have two Bay-area teams to choose from. Seeing the pictures and reading the story of the camp teams, I felt a reassurance, a testament to the spirit of baseball as something larger than feelings of anger, bitterness, hostility, or depression. And because baseball is the one sport I enjoy, I felt a connection, as though I had encountered one of Abraham Lincoln's "mystic chords of memory."

The other institution we visited was the Wing Luke Museum, named after Mr. Wing Luke, a rising star in the immigrant Chinese population of the 1950s and 1960s. He was a forward-looking man, perhaps even a visionary: the first "minority" to sit on the Seattle City Council, the first person of color to hold public office in the state, and a consistent champion of civil rights. Unfortunately for Seattle and possibly for the state of Washington, Mr. Luke was killed in a plane crash in 1965. He was still young, only forty—one of those proverbial comets that blazed a path exceptionally bright and short in the dark night sky.

The museum not only tells his story and honors his accomplishments but also gives historical background about the Asian groups who landed in Seattle—Japanese Americans, Filipinos, and Pacific Islanders—and either moved on and settled the western United States or stayed and built the city and the surrounding areas. Mr. Luke had been a champion of civil rights for all these Asians.

As we toured the museum, I mused about how Seattle had been and continues to be an important city for Asian Americans, despite war, forced removal, geographic trauma. The Asian American community there survived the loss of its Japanese American citizens in the 1940s and continues to thrive, albeit with a diminished Japanese American presence. Other groups of Asians have filled in.

For me, the most fun and nostalgic exhibit was one telling the story of Bruce Lee, Seattle's homeboy and my personal celebrity hero of the 1970s. He was such a star for young Asians who were sick and tired of the stereotyped

Asian male: short, bow-legged, buck-toothed, bespectacled, and obsequious, present only to be ordered around. Then, suddenly bursting on the scene was this irreverent, cocky, handsome kung fu master able to take on any crook or even a crowd of crooks and send all of them at once howling in pain, running for safety. After we watched Bruce Lee show off, the boys were cheering and strutting around, and all the girls were definitely in love. Martial arts studios in cities everywhere experienced a big spike in business. His early death was such a blow to young Asian Americans. Another blazing, short-lived comet.

I once had a friend who would use the expression "for a hot minute" where I would have said "for a split second." And for a hot minute, since that's what it felt like, I considered not going to the University of Washington to check out Dad's records. I had been doing everything and going everywhere on foot, since that was the only way to see the International District up close, to check out addresses and institutions and to get a feeling for the neighborhood. After several straight days of doing this, especially tramping up and down the hills, I was beginning to feel hot and tired. I was by myself, since Loren had returned home.

Thankfully, my hesitation didn't last for more than a hot minute or a split second, since my trip to the University of Washington was the cherry on top of the sundae. I shudder to think what I would have missed had I given in to hot and tired feet.

We kids had always heard that Dad had been a student at UW when the war broke out. When the forced removal became law, he, along with all the other young Japanese American men and women students, regardless of what class they were in—even seniors just months from graduation—were forced to leave school and go with their families into camps or other places outside the security areas along the coastal United States. While I never thought the story about Dad being a student there was a fabrication, I was never sure it was completely true because I had also heard that since Dad worked during the day, he went to classes at night. If this were true, I reasoned, maybe he had never registered as a legitimate UW student. When I called to make an appointment with the registrar, I was told just to come into the office and they would try to help me.

I caught a bus to the UW campus and followed the signs to the registrar's office. The campus looked lush and green, and I was tempted to wander around for a bit and check it out, but business first. I told myself that depending on how disappointed I was after my talk with the registrar, I could always stroll around afterward and even have some lunch on campus. Campus food used to be notoriously awful; I could see if things had changed from my days of eating on a college campus.

I found Schmitz Hall and walked through the open door into a light and airy office. I was lucky: no long line of impatient students waiting to be served. In fact, there was no one else waiting for anything. A young woman with dark hair, Christine she told me later, asked if she could help me. I told her what had brought me to her office. I wanted to know if she might be able to check and see if my father, George Kawamoto, had been a student at the University of Washington in the year the forced removal took place in Seattle, probably sometime in the spring of 1942. Would she even be able to locate records going back that far? I had my doubts. As I was talking to Christine, another young woman entered the office and Christine explained to her what I was requesting. Christine went back to her computer and the other woman disappeared momentarily. Christine found my father's name in no time and confirmed that he had been a student at UW at the time in question. I was impressed that she was able to access such information so easily. A moment to be grateful for technology, for not having to send someone down into a dark, dank basement to dig through boxes of old files with only the vague possibility of finding any proof or even any clues of my father having set foot on the campus. I was reflecting that it could have taken days, if anyone were even willing to do it, when the other woman reentered the room and placed something on the counter in front of me. I looked down to see a document with fancy black lettering bearing the official seal of the university. It was a bachelor's degree diploma. I saw that it had my father's name on it and burst into tears! How could this be? I knew he had never finished college anywhere, especially not here at the University of Washington. In fact, my parents had returned to Seattle only once or twice, many years after the exclusion, to visit a few old friends.

The two young women waited patiently for me to compose myself, then explained. Back in 2008, a large group of Japanese Americans, Nikkei as they are also called, put on what I will call an event, with the full cooperation of the university. They called it the Long Journey Home, a recognition and celebration of the many Nikkei whose educations were interrupted or came to a permanent end as a result of their forced removal from Seattle in

1942. The event included a ceremony in which the surviving Nikkei students who were able to be there were presented with official, honorary bachelor's degrees from the University of Washington. There were speakers and university officials, including the university president, in attendance. The planning committee, composed of members from the Nikkei community and various university departments, had diplomas made for every Japanese American student who had been attending the university at that time, a whopping 449 of them. Even those who were deceased or unable to attend the ceremony had a degree on file. That's how I came to receive my father's degree—the Office of the Registrar had kept it on file, perhaps hoping that someday, someone would come to claim it. I confess, holding my father's degree felt a little like some part of my journey, and his, had come full circle. I am so grateful to the Nikkei community of Seattle and to the University of Washington for creating this meaningful counterpoint, a small but meaningful dent into that bleak and dismal episode of our American history.

I know my dad would have loved to have finished college, and I also am pretty sure that he wouldn't have demanded that he go back to the University of Washington. Someplace closer would also have worked, since for him it was the mere fact of doing it, of being in that stimulating environment, of learning, of choosing what line of work, what profession would best suit his interests, skills, and goals. Of *getting an education*. Of *being* educated. I also believe that for him, the more education, the better. My sister once told me, much to my astonishment, that one afternoon she had heard Dad doing his understated version of bragging—about me getting my master's degree. He was outside in the yard chatting with a neighbor when he dropped that into the conversation. My parents never bragged about their children, never even talked much about us to anyone, so the magnitude of this tidbit of information did not escape me.

More than once in the stories that follow, I make reference to what a smart, intelligent, and talented individual my dad was. I tell about his artistic ability and his interest in music, even how as an adult he taught himself to play the piano. One story I heard growing up was that when he was around eighteen, he took a keen interest in photography and tried setting up his own dark room, but the room had no running water so he had to haul in buckets of water from another room to develop his pictures. I never heard that his efforts led to much of anything but the hard labor of hauling water. But for me the intrigue is that *he* was intrigued by the still developing artform.

I am left to ponder: What would my parents' lives have been like had they been able to remain in Seattle? More specifically, had they been able to live out their lives like an ordinary family in the International District of 1940s Seattle; to be surrounded and supported by a community of people who looked like them, who accepted them, who understood them. A community where no one had to explain themselves or their behavior to anyone else because they all knew what to look for, what to listen for, what all those little nuances of behavior and the spoken word stood for. They knew because they shared a common culture that bound them to an unspoken understanding of each other even in the subtlest of ways.

What if Dad had been able to finish college at the University of Washington and pursue the career of his choice—engineering or dentistry? If Mom had been able to raise her first daughter and the three of us who followed in the company and with the support of other young mothers, especially other Japanese American mothers?

Mom had been trained as a beautician and been practicing at a local beauty shop before the exclusion. Her beautician's license had to be renewed yearly, and Mary has copies of them dating from the late 1930s and staying current right up until 1942, when they end abruptly, never to be renewed. What if she had been able to continue renewing her licenses until *she* was ready to stop?

I will never know the answer to these questions. I can only do what I have always done: guess and imagine. So the stories that follow are factual when it comes to my own life, but in terms of my parents' lives, I am left to speak of them only as I experienced them in our lives together, until they were no longer here.

1

BATTLEFIELD TO BEET FIELD

The Germans Meet Dad in World War II

Reading the article for the first time flooded me with so many thoughts and memories and contradictory feelings that I was instantly overwhelmed. I didn't know whether my tears were of anger or dismay. It didn't seem to matter; they just came rolling down my cheeks and into the corners of my mouth. Tasting the salty tears and feeling at a loss for what else to do, I refolded the clipping along the faded crease lines and put it back in the envelope.

The title of the article is "Reunion," from a *New Yorker* magazine dated November 1991. My friend Jeanne had sent it to me those many years ago. I have a file cabinet filled with such items: little bits of poetry and artwork; photos of people, places, things, events; newspaper and magazine articles; cards and letters. All of them saved because they are intensely personal and precious or because they did for me what that article did: triggered some tender but densely layered feelings from my long-ago past, feelings too complex or painful to keep in the forefront of my memory. Feelings alluding to undefined memories or to past experiences that remained mysterious. So I did what I always do: I tucked the article away in my file cabinet in the folder marked "permanent." Like so much that was in that file cabinet, I knew it had another purpose in my life; I would just have to wait and see what surfaced.

My parents, married for sixty-seven years, died in 2000, within four months of each other. Not unusual, the doctor said, for couples who have lived together for so long. Since their passing, I have thought a lot about them and about our early lives on our Montana farm. My family left that farm in 1956, and we moved to Denver, Colorado, to be near my mother's family, to start our lives over yet again. By then we were a family of six—four kids and our parents—and I had started junior high school. Now when I look back at that country life, I am reminded of those old "cowboy and Indian" movies so popular in the 1940s and 1950s. But for us at that time, in that place, cowboys and Indians were not the good guys and bad guys in movies, not the chivalrous cavalry arriving at the last second to save the day from the marauding red savages; they were not legends of the Wild West or flashy movie stars. They were real people, just part of life growing up in the Montana of our childhood.

My family never chose to live on a farm. But less than three months after Japan bombed Pearl Harbor in December 1941, bringing the United States into World War II, President Franklin D. Roosevelt issued the orders: all Japanese Americans along the West Coast of the United States were to be removed from their homes and sent to incarceration camps. There were only the vaguest reasons flying about, including "national security" and "for their own protection." My parents and older sister were spared the terror and humiliation experienced by some of their friends, who answered a knock on the door only to be pushed aside by government agents marching into their home, interrogating the residents, and, without warning or reason, hauling the father or man of the family off to an unnamed jail. The rest of the family members were shipped off to a camp, and sometimes it was years before they were reunited.

Nevertheless, within the blink of an eye, the lives of my parents and sister were unalterably changed: they were evacuated from their modest Seattle apartment, leaving behind everything except what they could carry. My father lost his chance to finish college and my mother lost her supportive community of new, young mothers. They waved a bewildered goodbye to their possessions and their dreams and headed for Wyoming, which, as a state in the "interior of the country," was not considered a "security risk."

So, while the majority of the 120,000 persons removed were shipped off to incarceration camps located in desolate spots across the country, Mom, Dad, and my sister ended up in Sheridan, Wyoming, its own remote spot, with Heart Mountain incarceration camp not far away. They were allowed to go to Sheridan because Dad's parents lived there and could take them in. That is how my family avoided the camps and ended up on a farm.

I was born in Sheridan, but we didn't stay in Wyoming for long. The government was starting to release a trickle of Japanese Americans from the camps to grow food for the war effort. Much of the available farmland was in Montana. My dad, who had grown up in Sheridan, was finding it hard to get a job there. Even folks he had thought might hire him seemed to find some excuse not to do so. Montana seemed like a chance to have work as well as some independence, so he took advantage of the opportunity. Now it was the four of us, along with my grandparents, who headed for Montana. If Dad struggled with the irony of growing food for a government and a war that had just stripped him of all he had worked for, forced him from two homes, and sent him packing into the unknown, his wife and young children in tow, he never wasted time railing against the past; he just focused on the task ahead, which was to make the most of this new opportunity.

The passing of one's parents opens wide the door for all those questions never asked, the conversations never held. I was in one of those moods, missing my parents, wondering about them, wishing I had asked them—especially my dad, a reliable historian—many more questions about what it was like for him and Mom to have been so rudely, wrongly uprooted and forced back to Wyoming. And later how he felt being relegated to a lonely farm in Montana. That day, what spontaneously popped into my memory was the *New Yorker* clipping my friend Jeanne had sent me decades before. Suddenly there it was, separating itself from all the random thoughts and memories and regrets of the moment. I remembered, as I walked to my filing cabinet and retrieved the article, that it had been about Japanese Americans and World War II—but not about forced removal and incarceration. That latter story is no secret, but it is also not a story widely told or talked about. Only recently have school history books included a few paragraphs about this shameful episode in American history and then, not in all schools or all history books. But this short, modest article, tucked into the "Talk of the Town" section, revealed one of the best-kept secrets of World War II.

The piece describes an event that, on the surface, would appear to be rather prosaic: a breakfast party in San Francisco. But the host and guests seem an odd combination: San Francisco's Holocaust Oral History Project was hosting a "sushi and bagels" breakfast for the survivors of the all–Japanese American 442nd Regimental Combat Team, in particular the soldiers of Charlie Battery of the 522nd Field Artillery Battalion. Quite a few Americans have heard about the 442nd because, as the article states, it was "the most decorated regiment of the American military and the one with the highest casualties." Shortly after the war, the survivors of that regiment received many medals from the US government. But what made Charlie Battery special enough to the Holocaust Oral History Project for them to throw these soldiers a party?

It just so happens that the Japanese American soldiers of Charlie Battery, 522nd Field Artillery, were the soldiers who had liberated Dachau.

The article goes on to reveal a sordid government secret: the men of Charlie Battery had been threatened with court-martial if they ever revealed that they were the first American soldiers to reach Dachau and free its prisoners. The writer—unnamed, as all "Talk of the Town" writers were at that time—does not explain or analyze the reasons behind this threat. But they seemed obvious enough to me: How could our government extol such a moment of triumph if at that very moment it was holding Japanese American citizens, forcibly removed by the United States Army from their homes along the West Coast, in American concentration camps located all across the United States? How could it explain that some of those soldiers in Charlie Battery had been drafted directly from American concentration camps? It would surely be too much for the average mind to decipher and digest. Perhaps the officials told themselves once again that their suppression was in the interest of "national security," that people might act out, take to the streets, riot, burn, and loot. If so, this reasoning was, to my mind, pure rationalization, another way to justify the disgraceful, premeditated, unconstitutional act of rounding up innocent citizens, incarcerating them, and holding them without due process. So, to secure the secret with an airtight seal, our government threatened these honorable and supremely decorated soldiers with the dishonor of a court-martial.

The party for the remaining soldiers, according to the *New Yorker*, was a low-key, dignified tribute attended by several hundred guests, including about forty survivors of the Holocaust. The formal program consisted of a recognition of each of the two groups, soldiers and survivors. Then some people from each group rose to share their experiences of being in concentration camps, both German and American camps. The anonymous writer notes that the irony of one group of incarcerees freeing another group of incarcerees did not escape any of them.

The story the article quotes in greatest detail was one emotionally told by Janina Cywinska, sixty-two at the time of the party, who was Catholic, not Jewish, and had landed in Dachau because "her family was caught smuggling weapons to Jewish resisters." She is quoted as saying that she consciously tries not to think about "the horrors she witnessed" in the camp, but she will never forget "the day the Japanese-American soldiers handed her back her freedom." That day Janina, who was only sixteen, had been taken out along with others to be killed. They were standing side by side, blindfolded, waiting to be shot. They waited and waited but nothing happened. Finally, she whispered to the woman next to her, "Do you think they're trying to make us crazy, so we'll run and they won't have to feel guilty about shooting us?"

"Well, we're not going to run. We'll just stand here," her neighbor responded.

They continued to stand until Janina suddenly felt someone "tugging at my blindfold." He tugged in every direction until he finally "jumped up, because he was short, and he pulled it off." When she saw the Japanese man standing there, Janina said, she was convinced the Japanese had come to kill them, "and I didn't care anymore. I said, 'Just kill us, get it over with.'" In the moment, it seemed like nothing the soldier could say would convince her differently. Finally, the soldier "landed on his knees, crying, with his hands over his face, and he said, 'You are free now. We are *American* Japanese. You are free.'"

I had an uncle who was with the 442nd; he served in Italy. He survived the war and ended up dying at a respectable old age in Arvada, Colorado, a suburb of Denver. His widow, a friend of mine when we were both children growing up in Montana, has a small, narrow box containing his several war medals—three if the picture in my memory serves me correctly. During his lifetime, he rarely mentioned his time in the war, and I only figured out that he was in Italy because as an adult a memory came to me about a present he had sent us kids, his nieces and nephew, when we were on the Montana farm: a pair of small gondolas, one painted gold, the other silver. The boats were heavy, made of some kind of mysterious, soft metal that could be bent, and the color rubbed off on your hands when you played with them. Mom could tell we were intrigued by the soft, pliable metal as much as by the boats themselves. "Just hold and look. No bending," she admonished, "or you'll break them." But too busy to watch our every move, she couldn't stop us and just as she feared, they eventually fell apart—the bow and stern both bent to the right and left so many times that they finally fell off, leaving us with a strange, heavy metal lump. Even though we ended up destroying the boats, I cherish the memory of them and especially of my uncle who thought to send them to us from a continent away. We were so isolated on that farm, and we received so few presents, even at Christmas, that any gift seemed like a treasure.

Our farm was located in southeastern Montana, closer topographically to the plains of Kansas than to the beautiful, mountainous landscapes in the western part of the state, the part you most often hear about because of the movie stars and media celebrities who have ended up living there. We shared our flat, dry, nondescript corner of the state with the Crow Indians whose reservation was just a stone's throw from our farm in the Bighorn River Valley and from Hardin, the little town closest to us. The Crow had been scouts for General Custer at the Battle of the Little Bighorn, that famous victory for the Lakota Sioux and Cheyenne, who completely wiped out Custer and his entire Seventh Cavalry. Some of the Crow scouts went down with Custer. Mainstream Americans called this a massacre; the Indians called it the most famous Indian victory of the Indian Wars.

Unhappily, by the time we were farming in the Bighorn River Valley, there was nothing for the Indians to do on the rez, so drinking alcohol became a way of life and it wasn't unusual to see the men staggering around on the main street of our tiny town. My parents never said anything negative or nasty about the Indians; I think they understood what confinement on a reservation must be like because they understood incarceration camps and being sequestered on our Montana farm.

Cowboys—and cowgirls—also populated the valley, and some of those cowgirls were my grade school friends. They lived on big ranches and talked about driving cattle and roping calves and going to rodeos. But we lived on a farm, and farming sounds far less romantic and is always hard work. First, there is the weather, which the farmer has no control over but which can determine the financial outcome for the year. A bad dry year or a year with too much moisture could put even a hardworking, good manager in the red, and that might mean more than one year of digging himself out of debt. Then there are the growing seasons, which have their own lives, dictating to the farmer what he should do, when he should do it, and how much time he should take to do it. But whatever the season, there is always something that needs to be done. From seedling to harvest, plants need constant tending. On a farm, sick days are unheard of, and my dad—quiet, disciplined, and hardworking by nature—was not a man to complain. Back then, as a kid, I never thought about his health, but now I am sure there must have been days when he felt a cold coming on or was fighting something that was "going around" or was just plain tired. Those were probably the days when my mother expressed concern for him being outdoors for long hours in the hot sun or working late into the night, as he sometimes had to do.

Our two main crops were sugar beets and wheat; my grandparents raised an assortment of vegetables to sell to the locals. Dad farmed alone, making our farm one of the smaller ones in the valley. But to my child's eyes the fields were large, and to this day I can still envision them: long, straight row after row of young, green beet tops sprouting up. In between each pair of rows was a narrow, shallow trench to hold water, since in that part of Montana everything had to be irrigated. Sometimes those furrows played tricks on my eyes so when I looked down the rows, they eventually converged on a single, faraway spot, yet I knew this didn't really happen. I knew from playing in the fields that they actually went on in parallel lines, seemingly forever.

Along with the beets, weeds also sprouted up and needed to be taken out. Not an easy task. A man wielding a hoe with a long handle moves down the row, rhythmically scraping into the earth, pulling up the weeds, and thinning out the extra beet plants—making sure to leave just the right amount of space between the beets for them to grow round and fat. I know from hoeing short garden rows as a kid that that particular bend of the body is backbreaking. I couldn't help but be impressed by my grandfather, who could hoe with an almost entirely straight back.

A single man can't hoe acres of weeds by hand, no matter how good he gets at it. So weeding time is one time of year when a farmer needs extra help. I remember Dad bringing in "Mexican nationals" to help him do the hoeing. I don't know where or how he found these men or anything about them. All

I remember is that one morning I would look out at the fields and find them there, dotting the landscape, each at his own row, hoe in hand, an upright mark against an expanse of dark brown earth covered with spots of leafy green.

My older sister, the one evacuated with our parents when she was three, gave me a shock when she told me who else besides Mexican nationals had come to work on our farm. I was visiting her in Denver and we were sitting at her kitchen table, drinking green tea and reminiscing about life on the farm, something we never planned to talk about but always ended up doing ever since our parents' deaths several years earlier. Sharing memories about particular people and places usually led us to the same spot in the conversation: marveling at how different our lives would have been had we stayed on the farm. Sometimes our lives among cowboys and Indians, with the entire valley of the Little Bighorn River as our backyard, our lack of contact with other people outside of family and those at our tiny school—it all seemed almost surreal compared to our busy, crowded lives after we moved to Denver. It was during one of these conversations that Lilian told me that during the war years, the British had talked the United States into taking in German prisoners of war because they had run out of housing for them. She knew this for a fact because during a few of those terrible years, Dad had German POWs helping him hoe the fields.

When she told me this, I almost didn't believe her. It seemed too farfetched. The picture that popped into my head was like something from the theater of the absurd. Ionesco couldn't have done it better: fair-skinned, fair-haired, audacious German soldiers, now American prisoners of war. Young and physically fit, they are piled into the back of an open truck rolling down the highway to our farm. They are hanging over the sides, the wind rippling through their blonde hair as they squint into the sun or look down to watch the highway disappear dizzily beneath them. Perhaps they are tense and on guard, or perhaps they are feeling close to happy, just being outside the prison. Maybe they are singing some kind of German pop tune or a nationalistic war song as a sign of rebellion. The truck seems to cover so much open space before it finally pulls into a farmyard and jolts to a stop. They are greeted by a man, tan and fit, a little on the short side. All eyes are trained on him since the prisoners are eager to find out what's going to happen next. But wait a minute; even under the brim of his sweat-stained straw hat they can tell this man looks different—he's not a white man.

Whatever their previous mood, the prisoners are now stiff and alert, scanning. They watch and listen intently. As the farmer talks with their American guard, they can tell he speaks English. But is he an American? He looks suspiciously like one of those "Orientals" they have seen pictures of, mostly Japanese soldiers since Japan is Germany's ally in this war. But that alliance makes the Japanese enemies of the Americans. Yet this man isn't behaving like he's on the wrong side. His body language expresses confidence, as does his voice. He sounds like he's giving their guard instructions. In fact, he acts like he's the boss. How could he be Japanese? Maybe he's from China. They can't tell the difference. The prisoners become disoriented and fidgety. Who is this man? Who's in charge here?

My sister's voice brings me out of my imaginary flashback. I should ask her about facts, what she actually remembers, since the play I have constructed in my mind is pure fantasy. "What did they look like?" I ask. "How did they act?"

She doesn't remember specific faces but says, "They didn't wear those black-and-white striped prison uniforms like you always see in the movies. Their uniforms were drab and gray but not exactly what you'd think a prisoner would wear. And of course, they didn't speak English. They were with an American man who had a gun. He was their guard and translated for them." My sister was only around six or seven years old at the time, but she still remembers the guard for his rifle and the way it tinged the atmosphere with a shade of danger. "The guard had this large birthmark across his face." The memory seems to surprise her, and she hesitates, as if feeling a moment of sympathy for the guard.

Meanwhile, I am completely caught up in the moment, imagining the rifle and the guard and the birthmark. Forget the theater; this was more like a scene from film noir. "Go on," I prompt. "Then what?"

"Well, every day the guard would take a chair to some spot in the field, set it down, and just sit there all day long, his rifle across his lap. He kept his eyes peeled on the prisoners and watched them work the field." She doesn't think Dad ever had any trouble with the Germans, and as it turned out, German POWs across the nation gained a reputation for being well behaved and not inclined to attempt escape. Where would they go if they got out? The country was too big, too unknowable; besides, the American military, operating under the rules of the Geneva Convention, took good care of them—feeding them; keeping them clothed, warm, and dry; and giving them the opportunity to work outside the prison camps, often as paid farm labor.

It doesn't take long in my imagining for these German POWs to learn that on this farm, the short, fit, tan Asian man, my dad, really is the one in charge and that he is an American, a Japanese American. But does this news make the Germans feel relieved or more anxious and bewildered? How much do these men believe in the über-German, the Aryan master race, that superior white race whose dominance they had been fighting for? How do they feel about having to answer to someone so antithetical to that description? Maybe they don't care; maybe they haven't bought into the German propaganda. Maybe they are just young men who got caught up in the politics of the time, were drafted into the army, and were finally shipped into this tangled situation on an isolated farm in Montana's Indian country.

And they have no idea that my father, another victim of time and place and politics, had come within a hair's breadth of being in a prison himself—an American concentration camp. So he, too, found reprieve on a farm. That's why he is here today, greeting them. Knowing my father, I am sure none of the twisted irony of this scene escaped him. By my calculations, I was barely out of diapers at that time, but I wish I had been old enough to witness it, to see the look of wry amusement on Dad's typically impassive face.

So my father was never a soldier in the 442nd and never fought the Germans. He did not help liberate Dachau and did not win any war medals. And he never had to leave his farm to meet the Germans because one sunny summer morning after a hearty breakfast of bacon and his favorite eggs over easy, he left for the field and waited for the Germans to come to him.

2

A BETTER MOUSETRAP

I shudder to think what my life would have been like had I grown up an only child on our Montana farm. Outside of school, farm kids see very little of each other for obvious reasons, so I probably would have become a strange child who, spending so much time alone, would have had a terrible time relating to other children, perhaps to other people in general.

But lucky for me, I had siblings—two sisters, one older and one younger, and a little brother, the baby of the family. For those early years in our lives, we had each other to do all the things children do when they are growing up: play together happily and contentedly, go exploring around the farm or in the woods beyond our borders, do our farm and household chores, and sometimes fight with each other, though that didn't happen all that much and they were never serious fights or long-held grudges.

Those years were close and pleasant but it wasn't long before Lilian, four years my senior, began to pull away from the rest of us in her schoolwork and in the activities that interested her. She seemed to have more in common with her friends than with Mary and me, and with George she seemed maternal at times since she was ten years older than he was. Mary and I were much closer in age, so it felt natural that we continued to stick together for a much longer time. We had lots of adventures with each other but we don't have many pictures of them, so I have mostly piecemeal memories of what we did. But there is one particular memory so fond and amusing that I remember it clearly to this day, and it always makes me smile. It includes Mary, Grandpa, myself, and a mousetrap.

While my parents were busy growing sugar beets, wheat, and alfalfa, my grandparents—Dad's folks—were growing vegetables and had established a successful market garden. It seemed to me like people came from all over to get their beautiful fresh produce.

In the summer I remember "helping out" in their garden with my two sisters. I'm not sure how much actual help we were, but we did things like go with Grandpa to plant the seeds and add fertilizer; when the little green shoots started to spring up, we would get our hoes and dig out the weeds from around the plant. That was hard work, and I'm sure more than one plant lost its life to a careless hoe or a hoe not well controlled by young, inexperienced hands. A hoe slicing into the crust of the earth makes a particular scraping sound that is different from when the earth has already been churned up. It also feels different striking that crusty, untouched earth. That first slice of the hoe was always my favorite. Everything after that was just boring work.

When we weren't busy helping Grandpa with the garden, the three of us entertained ourselves by roaming the countryside, checking the creeks for beaver dams and watching for cranes or magpies, or playing some invented game in the farmyard. Sometimes these games would require us to use our toy Roy Rogers–style six-shooters so we could have shootouts outside the corral and die writhing, dramatic deaths; or maybe we would give each other a good soaking with our water pistols if it was a hotter than usual afternoon. One carefree day I said to my younger sister, who was probably around five at the time, which would make me seven, "I have an idea: let's go catch a mouse. I know how! First let's get some cheese and a long piece of string from Grandma."

Grandma was pretty much a soft touch when it came to anything her grandkids wanted, so when she asked why I needed so much string, I explained without hesitation that it was for my mousetrap. "A mouse? My goodness." The "my goodness" part was what she often said to us when we puzzled her or surprised her with our kid behavior. This time, as usual, that's all she said. No more questions asked. She just looked at me, shook her head, and handed me an extra-long length of fuzzy, tan-colored twine. Then she went to the fridge and broke off a piece of cheese from a larger slice of the ever-popular, ever-yellow Velveeta. She saw my excitement as I thanked her, and we hurried out the door, down the dusty road to the shed.

I have no recollection as to how I found the design for the mousetrap. It was the beginning of the 1950s, and Google was still light-years away. Television had barely made an appearance. It must have been in a book, or maybe I overheard some other farm kid talking about it. So, filled with unfettered confidence, I dragged my hesitant little sister up the dirt road to the tin shed. In my childish enthusiasm, I had no clue that my poor sister was terrified of mice. The way she clung to my hand and dragged her feet as we headed toward the shed should have tipped me off.

The tin shed was a large, Quonset hut–shaped structure with a corrugated tin roof—hence the name. Sometimes when we kids were caught in the rain, we would make a dash to the tin shed and wait out the storm inside. We were always a little awed by how big the rain sounded from inside, even when the drops weren't very big. When they hit the tin roof, they made a loud, sharp, heavy plunking sound; the heavier the rain, the louder the sound on the roof. Inside the shed, the dirt floor was mostly empty, which made the space seem even bigger. Along the sides were stacked odds and ends of equipment that Grandpa used for gardening—old empty bags, wooden crates of different sizes, bags filled with fertilizers and special soil, buckets, scoops, all kinds of garden paraphernalia. The space was perfect for catching a mouse.

I went to work constructing the trap while my sister hung back, watching me but sticking close to the door. I scouted around the sides of the shed for a shallow wooden crate, the kind that berries are sold in when you buy a flat. Then I found a short wooden stick, one fat enough to bear some weight, and carefully tied the string to one end. All the while my sister silently looked on. I went to the center of the vast, empty dirt floor and placed the cheese on the ground. Then, measuring with my eye, I placed the crate directly over the cheese and propped it up by placing the stick under one of the corners of the crate. Voila! The masterpiece was finished. Simple and efficient—something a child could make. The idea being, of course, that the poor, unsuspecting mouse, always on the prowl for food, would go for the tempting yellow cheese. Unbeknownst to him, I would be watching from outside through a crack in the door, and when I saw the mouse start to nose up to the cheese, I would pull the string. The box would slam to the ground, and the mouse would be trapped beneath it. Gleefully, I grabbed my sister's hand and dragged her with me to find our grandfather and show him my architectural triumph.

Within minutes the three of us—my sister, Grandpa, and myself—were creeping up to the door of the tin shed. I guess my sister was feeling safer with Grandpa now in tow. I had primed him for the sheer brilliance, the simple practicality, of my invention. The door was ajar and we could see clearly through the crack. Grandpa peered in and saw the trap bathed in a shaft of sunlight, the motes of dust floating above it. (It could have been a still life: *Mousetrap in Sunlight.*) He looked for several seconds before turning to me and saying with gravity and sympathy, "I think that mouse is laughing at you."

I was stung and shocked that Grandpa didn't see my trap the same way I saw it. I was also a little humiliated by his comment, but mostly I was disappointed. When I glanced at my sister to see how she was taking the news, she looked quite a bit more relaxed, more upbeat than before, even if she was trying hard to look sympathetic.

Maybe I was the only one who thought it would be fun to have a cute little pet mouse all my own. It never occurred to me to consider what my mother's reaction would be. I learned later that she, like my sister, was terrified of mice and would scream when she saw one. Clearly, she would never have let me through the front door carrying one.

Despite the lack of appreciation I received for my wonderful contraption, I hung around for awhile watching the trap, hoping Grandpa was wrong. After some time had gone by, feeling sad and dejected, I took a slow walk home, deciding that I would leave the trap up overnight to see if the cheese was taken. I did check the next day, but I don't remember if the cheese was there or not. I must have blocked from my memory the image that had been planted there: a mouse laughing raucously as it ran off with a pristine piece of Velveeta cheese.

3

MIND THE GAP

Locating Missing Memories

On my desk sits a smallish, round metal tin, about two-and-a-half inches in diameter. Painted on the top is an open red circle with a line through the middle. On the line are the words "Mind the Gap." The tin, now showing its age, sits on my desk to remind me of a trip to London where I first saw this symbol, without the words, as I was looking for an entrance to the underground, or the Tube as the locals call it. The symbol can be seen on signs all over London, and the stations to which they point—typically a very long escalator ride down—are crowded, clean, and well-lit. When the train pulls into the station and the doors slide open, a pleasant female voice coos "mind the gap." She is cautioning all passengers to be mindful of the narrow gap between the platform and the train.

The first time I heard this warning, I was both charmed and amused by it. It was so—British. I mean, really, Americans would never say to mind a gap. We are told to mind our parents, our teachers, our authority figures. We are told: "Look both ways before crossing the street," "Don't talk with your mouth full," "Don't talk to strangers," "Respect your elders," to name a few of the common rules most every kid has heard. We mind, or make an effort to mind, the adults who taught us these rules. But a gap? What's to mind in a gap?

In fact, I always resented gaps because I believed they had robbed me of important pieces of my family's history. I believed they were spaces I could never fill. But when I bemoaned this thought to a few of my friends, they surprised me by encouraging me to explore those spaces, to find out what I knew—and didn't know—about that space I was calling a gap. I might find that the gaps in my story, in my family's history, were as telling or possibly even more revealing than what was easily remembered. Maybe I needed to mind the gap or, more accurately, to mine the gaps.

My parents created a very large gap in my life by waiting until I was an older teenager, living in Denver, to mention why they had left Seattle for Wyoming all those years before—by waiting until then to say they had been forced to leave at the start of the war because they looked like the enemy. As a child on the farm, I knew that Mom and Dad lived in Seattle before my birth, but I never knew why they had left and I'd never asked. I had taken for granted that their move was a choice. When they told me, I was nearly an adult, and I was horrified and deeply discouraged that something like that—the direct result of overt, institutional racism—could have happened here in the United States. Where were the cherished tenets of equality, democracy, and the US Constitution itself? Where had they been? How did my parents feel about being treated so unjustly? Why had they never talked about this to us or to anyone? How had this act determined the rest of their lives—they were so young at the time? And how had it shaped the lives of my siblings and me?

At the moment when they revealed this shocking information, my parents not only filled in a gap I never knew existed—why they had left Seattle to become farmers—they also created a far larger one that now I felt compelled to fill.

Decades later, in my work as a psychotherapist, it became clear to me that one motivation for that kind of pervasive silence is trauma. Trauma is a very broad subject, but I would define it as something that happens in a person's life that is so deeply distressing, so shocking, perhaps so frightening that the aftereffects leave a deep mark on the psyche, a kind of scar that forms after the wound itself has healed. Psychologically, trauma causes traumatized people to protect themselves by repressing not necessarily the existence of the event itself but the memory of all the gory details that feed the trauma and give it its afterlife. In this way the person can, for the most part, put the trauma behind him or her—but it still lives on in the person's life even though she or he avoids consciously thinking of it. For traumatized individuals, it becomes very important to proceed with life as usual, to carry on as normally as possible, which helps put the trauma behind them. So the two work together in a kind of circular way: putting the trauma behind oneself and going on with life as usual, therefore forgetting about the trauma and putting it behind the person. Which is not to say that it really goes away. It just never really gets talked about. It gets buried, consciously repressed, but not defused. The nasty thing about trauma is that it can continue to do its dirty work long after the direct experience of the event.

Take the woman who has been raped. Rape is a heinous act, a criminal act in the United States and in much of the world, an act that leaves the victim traumatized. Yet even today the number of women who fail to report having been raped and do not get immediate help is alarmingly high. They often feel deeply ashamed that this has happened to them and too often feel some responsibility. They don't want to talk about it. They may not even confide in a friend or a partner. Even with the law on their side, they are aware of the times women have gone to the police or to friends or family who either don't believe them or question them about their behavior. What did they do to provoke the rape? What were they wearing? Did they protest or make it known that the man's behavior was not welcome? These and other questions or comments of this nature keep far too many women silent. Unfortunately, silence only makes them feel worse and combined with the trauma leads to depression, risky behavior like drug or alcohol abuse to tamp down the hurt, or acting out sexually to confirm any self-recriminating feelings they may be harboring. Even when those close to her know she is acting differently, a traumatized woman will often try to carry on with her "normal" persona.

Of course, the archetype of the trauma victim is the combat veteran, the person we imagine as suffering from the most extreme kind of trauma, for whom the posttraumatic stress disorder (PTSD) diagnosis was invented. After surviving his tour of active duty (we typically imagine the returning soldier to be a man), the veteran returns home but has trouble adjusting to civilian life. He doesn't want to talk about anything he has gone through. He is anxious, preoccupied, can't concentrate, has trouble connecting with people; when he hears a loud noise or anything that sounds like gunfire, he flexes into combat mode, ducking and hiding or pushing people around him to safety, or he becomes violent and destroys things around him. The people in his life, the ones who care, have to talk him into going to therapy where he must do the very thing he wants least to do: talk about his combat experience, tell the therapist the disturbing details, get the story off his chest, and try to develop a new perspective on the event(s).

As these classic examples demonstrate, acting like the traumatic event never happened, consciously excising it from one's life, or just wanting to move on and not talk about it creates a gap in a person's life where that experience took place. Those who know and care about the person eventually realize that something is missing in their understanding of him or her, and they begin to ponder the gap: What happened at the point in this person's story where suddenly there is a deep pocket of no information? What was going on before the gap and afterward, when the story picks up again? Where can one go to find out about that moment? Who does one talk to? How does one go about minding the gap?

These are some of the questions I ponder whenever I think of my parents and their story. I encounter so many gaps when I think of them. I fault myself for not having asked them more questions about everything pertaining to their lives, especially the years when they lived in Seattle with my older sister, just before they were evacuated to Wyoming. And even before that, before they were married, before they left their own families, before they were adults. What were their lives like? Where did they live? Where did they go to grade school? Did they like it; did they have friends; did the other kids treat them okay? What were their parents like and what kind of work did they do—was it by choice or because they had no choice?

I do know that my parents came from very different families. My mother grew up in a family with ten children; my father was an only child. He actually had a sister, but I think she died before he was born, so he grew up like an only child. How did my parents meet? At some point when I was a teenager, I learned that their marriage had been "arranged," and I was shocked that as late as the 1930s in America, such traditional customs still prevailed. I also heard that had either of them strenuously objected to the other person, the marriage would not have gone forward. But that information didn't matter when I grew older and realized that in a few important ways my parents were mismatched. When I saw their mismatch being played out, I would always say to myself, "Well, no wonder—they had an arranged marriage. People should stop that antiquated practice. Grrrrr!"

Trying to even partially answer these questions, trying to fill in some of the gaps in my knowledge of my family history, is a frustrating challenge since both my parents have long been gone and now my sister Lilian, the family historian, is also gone, leaving a gap not only in my history but in my heart. I just took for granted that I could always ask her questions whenever I felt like it. Now, unexpectedly, I am the eldest sibling, and I know I cannot count on my younger sibs to know what I don't know. At best, we can check with each other about our shared experiences, see if we can piece our memories together and come up with something resembling a picture we can collectively recognize. But what about those other gaps, the ones none of us knows anything about? Maybe I should start with myself and figure out what I do know and then see where the gaps lie.

I used to say, whenever anyone asked me about myself, that my life really began when my family moved to Denver. But I was already in junior high school at that point. So what happened to those first twelve or thirteen years of my life, that extensive gap of time?

As a teenager and a young adult, I didn't want to think of, let alone own, my early years on a poor farm in rural, isolated Montana. For me, because of our poverty and isolation, those years were not only physically hard and demanding, they were also shameful. I tried not to dwell on what we didn't have. I focused mostly on going to school, being a good student, having a friend there—and when I was home doing my chores and my homework if I had any and having fun with my sisters. It's not that I was unaware that most of the other Japanese American farmers in our valley were better off than we were. They had been there longer and were established farmers. We were the newcomers from the city, plopped down on the farm as a result of circumstances beyond anyone's control. I could tell when we visited the other farm families that their houses were bigger and in much better shape than ours. They had more farm equipment parked in their yards; they had indoor plumbing and nice kitchens and bathrooms and decent furniture in most of their rooms—at least the ones we were allowed to see. I could see all these differences, but for some reason they didn't make me feel personally inferior to my classmates or friends. Possibly because I was always a good student who loved school—so my teacher really liked me—and because I got along well with the other kids, I didn't focus on or pay much attention to the material deficits of our home life. Also, kids in our grade school, before video games, iPads, and all the fancy tech devices, tended not to relate to each other based on what we had and could bring to school to show off to the other kids. Recess was usually a time to play games, group games like baseball and tag.

When, as a searching young adult, I encountered Buddhism, its general tone felt familiar to me. At the time I thought that might be because of child-hood memories of my grandmother, Dad's mother, but I realize now that the familiarity went deeper than that. My childhood in Montana, as I think about it now, was all about living in the present moment, as I understand Buddhism challenges the practitioner to do. On our farm, that's what life was like; we went day to day, doing the chores that seemed well defined. They were not metaphorical or intangible or intellectual exercises. They were solid tasks requiring physical activity. No one sat at a desk typing or going over papers with pen or pencil or scribbling things on a chalkboard or butcher paper. There were no dreaded, endless meetings, no phones with multiple blinking buttons.

The association of Buddhism with Grandma was real. I joke about inher-iting the search-for-religion gene from her. Just in the years that we lived near her in Hardin, she must have tried out several different Eastern religious sects. At the time I didn't know that they had different names since they all seemed to include chanting, bowing, clapping, and honoring ancestors. But no matter what practice Grandma was trying out at the time—Buddhism, Shintoism, or something I'd never heard of—every evening before dinner, she never failed to take the first bowl of rice, steaming and patted into a smooth mound, to Kami-sama, to God. She would place the bowl in front of a modest shrine on her chest of drawers, put her hands together in prayer mode, bow and mumble something, then hurry back to the kitchen to fin-ish serving dinner. Sometimes, if asked, I would do this ritual for her, sans the mumbling.

But she wasn't the only one in the family doing rituals. During most of the year, Dad would rise around dawn, and the day would kick into the mode of full steam ahead. Even before breakfast he was outside feeding and tending to the sheep, cows, and pigs. Mom would be up shortly after him, making breakfast and getting us kids up and moving and ready for school. After a hearty farmer's breakfast—bacon or ham or sausage, eggs and toast, and strong black coffee—Dad was back outside, working in the fields or repairing a piece of farm equipment or taking care of some other need in the farmyard. We kids would be heading for school, my older sister in the yellow school bus that took her to the school in town and my younger sister and me going with Mom, who had to drive us to our nearby, one-room country schoolhouse. Our baby brother, years away from school age, had to go along for the ride. In the fields, Dad would be doing whatever the season required: plowing the land and planting in the spring, tending the crops in the summer, harvesting in the fall. All labor-intensive work. All never-ending. That is, until the winter, when Montana temperatures didn't hesitate to drop below freezing and the ground, trees, buildings, anything left outside would be covered with snow—sometimes a thin dusting, other times large drifts and piles, rippled and patterned by the wind. Then life quieted down some and took on a slower pace, but even in winter, animals and anything else that was alive had to be fed and secured. That included us kids as well.

It was in the winter that we kids could actually spend some pleasant time with Dad and that sometimes we could do things as an entire family. I remember one winter when we got a Monopoly game, and together we spent many frigid evenings next to the living room heater, the game spread out on a card table unfolded strictly for that purpose. Mom would pop a huge mound of popcorn and coat the snowy kernels with salt and our farm-fresh churned butter. The board eventually became stained from everyone's greasy, butter-slick fingers rolling the dice and advancing the little figures, trying not to get stuck in jail for the better part of the game while everyone else was purchasing real estate with that colorful paper money. We had a blast! That was the only time we had a taste of what it was like to have money, to make lots of money, to spend it carefully or recklessly, or to lose it altogether.

It was on our farm that I first heard another proverb that stuck with me: Fathers work from sun to sun; mother's work is never done. It is true. The work of mothers—taking care of the myriad household tasks that have to be done all over again the next day and the next and the next, on top of raising the children—is one of endless duties. And it is also true that until winter takes over and nothing can grow, farmers work in an endless cycle that can include waking in the middle of the night not only to handle animal emergencies but also, in our valley, to manage concerns like irrigation that I don't really understand even now.

Given this type of lifestyle, spending time just sitting back and quietly pondering one's feelings was not something a farmer had much time for. I think farming is mainly about survival—not only of yourself but of the plants and animals you are responsible for because, ultimately, they are responsible for you as well.

I don't remember ever hearing my father complain—not when I was a child or when I was an adult. He was someone who just saw what needed to be done and did it. So it was never from him that I came to think of their forced removal from Seattle in 1942 as a traumatic experience. In fact, neither he nor my mother ever talked about living in Seattle, leaving Seattle, the war with Japan (or Germany), or why they were living in Wyoming with Dad's parents when I was born. They never said why they left Wyoming soon afterward to go to Montana, to a farm equally, if not more, isolated than the one in Wyoming. And I never asked either one of them any of those questions. I was just living my life on a farm, in a shabby little house, and going to a tiny country school outside a small town in Montana. That was just the way it was. That is the way trauma works.

I have only the vaguest memory—not even a real memory, just barely a whisper of a memory—about the moment when I asked my mother if the United States had gone to war with Japan. I was still in grade school and my teacher—our teacher, as she taught all six grades in our school—had made some comment of which I have no conscious memory, but whatever she said had made me highly suspicious that she was referring to a war with what sounded like Japan. I remember being surprised and hoping it wasn't true. I didn't like the way it was making me feel inside—a little afraid, but not exactly sure of what. That evening I asked my mother, "Mommy, did the United States go to war with Japan?" She looked at me as though she was surprised I didn't already know that, and then she affirmed my fear. Yes, indeed we had. I don't think of myself as a person who has encountered dramatic, life-changing moments, but thinking back, perhaps that could be called one. I remember that I went to school the next day feeling extremely self-conscious, although no one was treating me any differently than they had the day before. I was the one who was feeling different.

I think everyone, including the kids in my grade school, knew that the United States had been in a war. It was in the past, we knew, and lots of countries like France, England, and Germany had participated. Not that the subject ever came up at school or in conversation with friends. We all knew that war was not a good thing overall, but it also didn't seem like a particularly big deal; otherwise, wouldn't folks be talking more frequently and loudly about it? We also knew there were statues of soldiers and other kinds of war memorials located all around the country. We had seen pictures of them. The pictures of soldiers I most vividly remember are the formal wedding pictures of some of my family's Japanese American farm friends, young couples who would become the parents of my friends. The radiant bride and proud groom are standing together facing the camera; the bride is wearing a fancy, floor-length, white wedding gown with the long train draped in a precise semicircle around the feet of both bride and groom. The groom is dressed in his United States Army uniform. Later, as an adult viewing the pictures and trying not to be cynical about the military, I posited (only to myself) that while those fancy wedding dresses were expensive, the men could avoid paying for a tuxedo or a dress suit because they already had their army uniforms. All they had to do was see that they were washed, starched, and ironed, and they would be dressed for nearly any occasion—including their weddings. I had no idea until much later in my life how proud the Japanese American soldiers were of serving in the US military—serving their country in our war against Japan.

But did any of us, my classmates in Hardin included, have any idea about the true horrors of war, about the death and dying that surrounded those directly involved and the consequences of each loss to the families and loved ones? I doubt it because no one ever talked about the war. I don't even remember any gossip about anyone's uncle, father, or friend having been killed in the war. Surely, some of the families in the area had lost loved ones somewhere during that global conflagration, but their losses, grief, and trauma remained buried with their loved ones. That's why I was so stunned when Mom told me that the United States had been to war with Japan. Thinking back on who was farming in our valley, I now recall not only the Japanese names but also a number of German last names. Everyone had probably engaged in a silent pact to leave that subject alone and move on.

I can't be sure, but I think it was my big sister, Lilian, who must have told me about the American concentration camps for the Japanese Americans. I must have said something to her about our being at war with Japan, how shocked I was to find that out. Lilian had been with my parents when they were evacuated from Seattle, so she knew about the war and the exclusion firsthand, although she would have been too young to really understand what was happening and why. She was barely three when they were forced to leave their home. She probably felt the tension in the air, saw her mother's distress, watched as everything around her—including her toys and extra clothes—was put in boxes and given away or packed up to be stored somewhere. She saw her home disappear behind her as she held Mom's hand and they turned their backs and walked away. I hope she was holding fast to her favorite doll, Alice, to give her solace in the midst of the chaos going on around them. So even if she couldn't have told anyone then what was happening and why, the experience was being embedded within her, leaving a deep mark on her young psyche. But afterward, like my parents, she never talked about that time or openly asked our parents questions about what had happened. The war had created gaps for everyone, it seems. No one ever seemed to mention it, and no one ever talked about the forced removal and incarceration. Two seminal events in American history, and they seemed never to have taken place. To me now, it's clear that that's another example of what trauma does, how it stops the mouth and even erases memories.

Before World War II, my parents had been part of Seattle's large and thriving Japantown, the Nihonmachi, living in an apartment building that was either owned or operated by Japanese people with whom they had become fast and lasting friends. I don't know for certain what my father's plans were as a young man, but the snippet of the story I have heard is that he worked during the day and went to classes at night, at the University of Washington. One of his day jobs, perhaps the only one, was as a janitor in a building that housed what sounded like artists or maybe bohemians. One resident was either an opera singer or a teacher of opera, and through this person—I don't know whether a she or a he—Dad was introduced to music. He heard classical music, opera, and—I want to believe—the pop music of that era, the big bands like Duke Ellington, Count Basie, Benny Goodman, Jimmy Dorsey.

This love of all music and his scant musical training would surface later in our lives when Dad taught himself how to play chords on our piano and then to add the melody with his right hand. He got very good at playing popular songs with this technique. However, despite his dedicated interest in music, it turned out that Dad was not naturally musical. It seemed like he lacked a sense of musical timing, of rhythm, so whatever he played seemed slightly off the beat. To his credit, he never cared. He just sat down and played whenever he could. I had always thought it was Mom who practically demanded that we get a piano so we kids could take lessons and learn a musical instrument, a sign of culture and breeding in her eyes, I'm sure. But maybe it was Dad who put the bug in her ear. At least we know he never protested, and even in the poverty of our farm life, we had an old but standard upright piano taking up more than its share of space in our small living room.

My younger sister, Mary, has a few original documents in her file drawers that reveal more about our parents' Seattle lives. She has our mother's official licenses to work as a beautician, a "beauty culturist" as it is labeled on the license. Apparently, Mom did this work for some years; Mary has license renewals for the years 1938 through 1942, until the exclusion. I never questioned how my mother seemed to know how to cut our hair so expertly, separating it into sections on our heads, having shears that were used solely for cutting hair, knowing how to cut the hair not just with a blunt cut along the bottom but to expertly layer it with a kind of scraping up-and-down motion on one small sheaf of hair at a time. I watched her do this and years later tried it on college friends who didn't want to pay a lot of money for a professional cut. (I shiver to think of my chutzpah!) No one's hair came out looking alarmingly hacked up. Thankfully.

Lilian was born in Seattle, but not until my parents had been married for years. I don't know why they waited so long, whether the wait was intentional or indicated some sort of difficulty or was a question of finances or if one parent was reluctant to have children for whatever reason. Between Lilian and me was another four years, followed by Mary two-and-a-half years later and our brother, George, another two years after Mary. At last, the long-awaited male. Although, knowing my father, I doubt if he made a big fuss over not having had a son early on. From the very beginning, he was an enlightened male, possibly because his mother was such a strong, interesting, and independent woman.

Dad's mother, early on, had several of her own businesses, including a barbershop and a restaurant; by the time we kids knew her in the late 1940s and early 1950s, she could be found working alongside Grandpa in their big vegetable garden. Raising and selling their vegetables was their livelihood when we were growing up. But to me, the most impressive thing I heard about this grandmother was that she had divorced her first husband, Dad's biological father. The story goes that Mr. Kawamoto, Dad's father, wanted to return to Japan after having spent some years in America. I don't know why. Whatever the reason, Grandma was having none of it. She was smart, resourceful, and apparently enjoying her freedom of mobility and her independence—things she knew she would have to give up if she went back to Japan. Women in Japan in the early 1900s were not experiencing the kind of freedom American women were, as limited as it would seem from our contemporary perspective. So she chose to remain in the States. I am assuming that they agreed on a formal divorce so her husband could remarry free and clear if he chose to do so. That is speculation on my part; for all I know, Grandma may have been the one to demand the divorce so she could remarry. That would not surprise me. I know her reasons were practical ones, but I am still in awe of her for making the choice to remain behind, a single woman—rather, a divorcée—with a young child, my father. Divorce in those days was frowned upon even in America. Given those circumstances, she needed her skills, her drive, and her resourcefulness to take care of herself and her son. From what I can piece together, that is where her business ventures—the barbershop and restaurant—came into the picture. The happy ending to that part of her story is that Grandma did eventually remarry—to the only man we kids grew up knowing as our grandpa, Grandpa Saito. As kids living around them, we took for granted that they were happy together, and today my sister Mary is the first to mention how well they got along and how they seemed to live their lives as a team.

Another thing about Grandma that I took for granted and never asked her about was that she was well educated, I'm guessing especially so for a woman of her generation. She could read and write in Japanese and had learned from necessity to do so in English. Not all Japanese immigrant women of her generation had forced themselves to learn enough English to operate a business or to speak to their grandchildren. When we kids made the short walk from our farmhouse to hers, we would always see magazines and sometimes thick paperback books in Japanese strewn around her living room. She also subscribed to one or two standard magazines in English. I have a vivid image of the *Reader's Digest*, small and easy to carry around. It came so frequently that there was always a stack of them piling up somewhere in the living room. We knew she kept a journal in Japanese, and it was at her house that we first saw those accordion-folded blank Japanese books. She used them to keep her journals.

Grandma had refined taste in clothes, food, and furnishings. When we kids knew her, she never had an excess of money, and there weren't many places for her to go where she could get dressed up. But she kept herself up by keeping her hair done and her clothes clean, presentable, and fashionable. Often, her most stylish dresses were the ones she had sewn herself. We knew she had always liked clothes a lot, and we had seen pictures of her as a much younger woman dressed in fur-collar coats and the hats and dresses of the latest fashion. And we noticed that whenever she left the farm to run an errand, she would put on lipstick and powder her face. Grandma was a fearless driver, and she drove herself and sometimes we kids anywhere the situation required. She liked cars and appreciated them for making her life easier to navigate, but more interesting to me is that she seemed to appreciate how they looked—as with her clothes, she liked a fashionable-looking automobile.

Her kitchen and living room furniture, we were warned by our parents, was high-end and of excellent quality, even though I never particularly cared for how it looked—overstuffed chairs and what I was told was an expensive, horsehair-stuffed couch with leather upholstery. She later bought a cloth-covered couch, which I liked much better. As a consumer she somehow seemed to keep up with products, from kitchen appliances to the latest dress fabrics. I especially remember her large, roomy, well-lit refrigerator—undoubtedly the newest model, as I'd never seen anything like it. We kids would peek inside as often as we could, reaching in to get a single carrot or radish or whatever we could find to snack on. Opening and shutting the door, watching the steam enter the room as the cold air collided with the warm air—I think it drove Grandma nuts because she could see her electric bill go up and up each time the door let out its current of cool air. It was Grandma who had the old-fashioned, hand-cranked Victrola on which we could play heavy, easily broken 78-rpm records—both Japanese and American. So while we kids didn't really appreciate the value of these details about our grandmother, we nevertheless were absorbing the benefits of her tastes and lifestyle.

After our move to Denver, Mom also had to work outside the home and Dad—sometimes working more than one job—never hesitated to do laundry, cook meals, help with the housework, and iron the occasional shirt. He didn't seem to give any of it a second thought. We kids got used to coming home from school late in the afternoon and seeing Dad in an apron cooking the evening meal. It wasn't until we girls became young women that we realized what an anomaly our father was: most fathers and, indeed, most men of our own generation had never set foot in a kitchen, let alone picked up a clothes iron.

I am guessing that my mother never got over the forced removal and what it ultimately deprived her of. I don't know for sure, but I think my parents' lives in Seattle were not very different from those of many young urbanites living fairly ordinary American stories: going to work, raising small children, perhaps going to school—adult education or college—part-time. My parents didn't have a lot of money, but from the few pictures I have seen of them at that time, they didn't appear poverty-stricken: they always looked clean and well-groomed, their clothes were simple but well kept, and in one picture Mom is sitting in a large overstuffed armchair, holding a few-months-old Lilian, and there is a bookcase in the background. The bookcase must have been my father's doing, as we always had one, even on our farm. In Seattle, they socialized with other couples and families whenever they could; in the manner of the day, they dressed for the occasion when they went out to movies, on picnics, to visit friends. It tickles me to see my young, handsome father and my even younger, very pretty mother in their stylish dress-up clothes—Dad in slacks with small pleats at the waist, Mom always in a dress and heels. They were a good-looking couple. They had a life, and it looked like they were enjoying it.

Being banished to a farm in Wyoming practically overnight must have felt to Mom like being sent to Mars or the moon. Everything would have looked different—no big buildings, no streets or sidewalks, no streetlamps, no department stores or corner markets. And no friends. Hardly any people around in tiny, rural Sheridan. In fact, hardly any Asian faces except for my grandparents. At least that's the impression I got after hearing how hard it was for Dad to find work after they arrived in Sheridan. None of the white businessmen or farmers would give him a job. Mom, in her heart, was a very social being, and I'm sure she was bereft at having to leave her friends behind, especially her support group of new moms. And the city lights and all the city things they were used to doing with their friends who lived down the hall or around the corner or down the street.

Mom's only support in Sheridan was Grandma, Dad's mom, and I have never heard of a time when they got along. I never knew how Grandma felt, but I learned early on that Mom resented Grandma and felt demeaned by her. Close to tearing up, Mom would tell us that Grandma controlled everything and ordered her around and made her do things the way Grandma wanted them done. I don't believe that Grandma yelled at Mom or was abusive or violent to her in any physical way. That was not her style. Could she be bossy? Absolutely. She was used to calling the shots and doing things her own way. And I am pretty sure she didn't treat Mom like an equal. It was only years later that I discovered that in Japanese culture it was traditional for a young couple to live with the husband's parents after they were married, at least for a while. In that setting, the mother-in-law ruled supreme and didn't hesitate to treat her new daughter-in-law like a servant. It was up to the new wife to acquiesce to being ordered around and doing much of the housework. Those were the rules, everyone knew them, and everyone played their part. I don't think anyone bothered to inform my American-born mother about the Old World expectations of a daughter-in-law. If she knew them, she might still have resented them, but perhaps she wouldn't have taken my grandmother's behavior toward her so personally.

By the time I was old enough to observe interactions between my mom and grandmother, Grandma must have toned it down quite a bit, since she always seemed to me to be civil and respectful of Mom, and Mom would respond stiffly but in-kind. I guess I would say that while there was no love lost between them, they did maintain a stilted politeness.

My parents were among the large group of Nisei, second-generation American-born citizens, who were evacuated from Seattle. The operative word here is "citizens." Whatever racism or prejudice they had encountered up until that point in their lives, it had given them no indication of how deep those feelings could go and how drastic the consequences would be for them. Even today, it is shocking for me to consider our government deciding to toss aside the US Constitution and proceed with rounding up second- and third-generation American citizens en masse and incarcerating them in specially built prison camps. It sounds more like the Russian gulag than our American democracy. Especially since these individuals had been accused of no crime and assumed, right up until they were boarding trains to the concentration camps, that they would have full recourse to whatever protections were afforded citizens under the US Constitution. I can have the luxury of outrage, viewing the events from the distance provided by history; but for my parents, sister, and all the others, what they experienced was pure trauma, the kind imbued with an oppressive dose of cultural shame and dishonor—feelings that added a heavy lock to a door already closed tight to any future discussion.

In the unexpected moment of trauma, the task is to get through it, to survive it. After that, the task becomes carrying on with one's life, putting the trauma—the rape, the forced removal, the escape from fire or flood, or whatever the disaster—behind one and getting back to "normal" as quickly as possible. This was certainly true for my parents. It served them no obvious purpose to talk about their bad fortune, their precious losses, their psychic humiliation, the daunting work of starting their lives over again, empty-handed. Their task was just to do it. Besides, talking about it only took them back to those fearful and confusing moments—and those moments and that time were to be avoided as much as possible. Some might label this denial, but I maintain that they were not so much engaging in denial as they were carrying on against the odds, focusing on the positive work of life and not getting bogged down by anger and bitterness, by the negative—in other words, making their lives count. They had experienced what it was like to be treated as if they did not count, as individuals or as people in general. It is much to their credit that they didn't take on that behavior.

But, of course, the tradeoff for their inability to talk about what happened is that they created gaps in their story, and the gaps are what the rest of us are left to deal with.

After we left Montana when I was starting junior high, I never looked back, and I never went back until the mid-1960s, for my grandfather's funeral. I was twenty-three, and Grandpa's death was the first major loss in my life. Grandma was still there, alive and quite well, much as I remembered her except a little grayer. She still had a lot of energy and an active mind. My sisters and I took a walk around their farmyard, and it seemed that not much else had changed either. I don't remember many details about that visit except the poplar trees. When we were still kids, Grandpa had planted a row of what I called silver poplar trees because of the silver color on one side of their leaves. There were four young trees, planted alongside an irrigation ditch filled with water on the edge of the yard and bordering a field. That's what I remember. The important thing was that someday they would grow tall and give the yard some much-needed shade—the farm was on the plains side of the state, flat and dry and not endowed with many trees. Being a child, impatient and curious, I wanted them to grow fast, to get tall right away so I could see what they would look like and so they could do their job. To see them that day, tall, silver-leafed, fully grown, not only fulfilling Grandpa's wish for shade trees but also being a clear, vivid, material reminder about the passing of time—and of life itself—I was flooded with a moment of grief and nostalgia and gratitude.

Grandma and Grandpa had continued to live in the same little house, doing only the basics to keep it up. Grandpa's hothouse was still there, too, but now devoid of seedlings. Grandpa's hothouse was really a tightly closed shed with walls of plastic sheeting to retain heat and moisture, which would accelerate the growth of the sprouting plants. He started out his seeds in those tiny square containers one sees at supermarkets in the springtime, sporting their nascent vegetable or flower shoots, the containers city dwellers purchase for their potted urban gardens. At some point, when Grandpa deemed that the new sprouts were ready, they would be transplanted into the big garden outside. On the day of my return, the hothouse was warm inside but not at all moist, and it was empty of anything live except a sense of Grandpa's spirit. He was virtually the only person who ever went inside it. Even now, I can almost feel what it was like whenever I had to enter the hothouse. I was immediately immersed in the heavy, humid air, almost too thick to breathe. It usually gave me a moment of panic before my breathing could adjust from the dry Montana air outside to the almost tropical environment inside.

Grandma stuck it out there for a few more years by herself on the farm before she moved to Denver to live near my parents. Her physical body remained quite strong, seasoned by working the land, growing vegetables, and running her business. But her mind declined and deteriorated into what we now call dementia. I didn't see much of her, as I was living in the Bay area. But I do remember a few visits that demonstrated the scourge of her dementia, conversations in which she would confabulate detailed stories about whatever was convenient in the moment, like that man standing over there—pointing to a perfect stranger—and what he was doing or how she had known him in the past and what he used to do. She could look and sound utterly convincing, except that none of what she was saying had any basis in truth.

Many years after Grandpa's funeral, in the mid-1990s, I made one last visit to Montana, to the old homestead. I was with my husband, who was curious to see where I had spent my childhood. I had tried to describe to him the vast emptiness of the Montana plains, that feeling of remoteness from the rest of the world, my childhood farm, and our life of rural hardship. He couldn't quite imagine what I was talking about and wanted to see it for himself. By this time, I wasn't sure just what I would find or what I could show him that had anything to do with my life. It had been nearly forty years since my family had left there.

But we decided to go anyway, to take a road trip over the Rockies and through Wyoming into southern Montana. The mountain country is truly beautiful and we reveled in the scenery—the jagged snow-covered peaks, the pine-covered lower slopes, and the rolling foothills smoothing out onto the flatlands that slide into the vast plains of the Midwest. But before we headed into those dry plains, my husband insisted that we go through Sheridan, the town in Wyoming where my parents had landed after exclusion, where I was born, and where my father had gone to high school.

I had forgotten, or at the time was too young to realize, how pretty Sheridan is. It is a small town that does not have that look of the scraggly desert outpost, the Pony Express pick-up-a-fresh-horse-and-keep-moving look, the gritty Tombstone of the movies. The stereotype folks imagine when they think of Wyoming. In Sheridan, the mountains form the backdrop to a town that looks friendly and green and clean, if not small and contained. We strolled along the main street, short but more interesting than those of most small towns, probably because of its old, authentic-looking Western storefronts that clearly had been there for many, many years and been kept up with pride. Strolling along so as to take in as much as possible, I was suddenly stopped in my tracks by a large, intricate neon sign on the front of a bar, sticking out well over the sidewalk. I felt like I knew that sign and for a moment I was in a flashback, back to being a very young child who loved to watch the cowboy on the bucking bronco holding firm to his wild ride. The sign flashed consecutive positions of the cowboy on his horse, moving from one position to the next so that when you stood and watched for a few seconds, the rider really seemed like he was on a bucking bronco. I couldn't believe my eyes. The sign was still there. The place was called the Mint Bar, and if we hadn't gone in and had something to drink, we'd have missed an opportunity to hang with the locals.

To my regret, I had no idea where my grandparents' old house was or where their farm had been situated. So we went instead to the high school, the one Dad had attended and graduated from. It was nondescript, of light-colored stone, and not very big. My husband, Jan, insisted on taking a picture of me sitting on the front steps. He thought it would be a nice tribute to Dad, but what seeing the school gave me was an even deeper appreciation for my father's native curiosity and deep desire to learn. It was clear to me that in a school that size, in a town that size, at a time when teaching covered pretty standard topics, Dad's interests could not have been satisfied. He had needed to pursue his quest for more knowledge on his own, to forage around as best he could to keep the light alive, to not abandon his desire to keep learning. It would have been the easiest thing in the world just to give up, especially after moving to Montana. But even then, Dad maintained his desire and determination to keep his curiosity from being blunted, to keep alive his personal torch of knowledge.

Sheridan was a good place to visit first, since it turned out to be emotionally not that difficult. But I was anxious about moving on to Hardin. What would we find there? I knew there would be lots of changes, but I couldn't imagine what they would be. I didn't expect the rundown little building we'd called home to still be standing, unless it had been turned into some kind of shed or outbuilding. Would my grandparents' home still be there? Would anyone be living there? Would my old country schoolhouse still be standing? Would there still be fields of crops, and what would they be? Would we be able to find anyone I had known growing up? And what about the town itself, tiny Hardin with its one short Main Street and a competition between who had more buildings—the churches or the bars. In our day, the churches outnumbered the bars by only one, and the rumor was that that was the law: a town could not have more bars than churches. And for a town of well under 3,000 people, the number of each was phenomenal: thirteen churches to twelve bars! I cannot swear to those exact numbers after all these years, but both numbers were in the double digits.

The gravel county road branching off the main highway about ten miles out of town was still there, and we took it just like we had in the old days, hoping it would again lead to my former farmhouse. It didn't because the quarter-mile dirt lane branching off the county road to our yard no longer existed. There was no sign that it had ever existed. It was covered over by a medium-sized field that bordered the road and extended down at least as far as where our house had once stood; how far beyond that, we couldn't tell. I can't say I was surprised. The house was nearly ready to go when we lived there, but I wasn't expecting it to be replaced by a field. The land where the barn and shed and corral and all the living, by people and animals, had taken place somehow didn't seem fit to be planted. The earth underneath had always felt too dense and tightly packed for tender seed buds to push their way through. But here they were, young plants in straight rows, looking healthy and green. Probably sugar beets. I knew a little about what it must have taken to prepare that patch of land for growing plants. Hard work and faith in the ability of the land to regenerate would be my guess.

The longer lane on the opposite side of the road was still there, as was the field, and we could see Grandma and Grandpa's little house outlined against the afternoon sun. We turned into the lane, and on the way up to the house we saw a farmer in the field. Jan braked to a stop, hopped out of the car, and waved the man down. He made his way over to us and gave us a quizzical look. Clearly, we weren't from around here, and clearly, we weren't farmers.

The conversation turned out to be polite, pleasant, and a bit informative. The man now farming the land did not know many of the names I asked him about, of the other Japanese American farmers who had the neighboring farms when I was growing up here. But he did remember hearing Grandpa's name, Fred Saito. He seemed to know that the Saitos had once owned the house at the end of the lane we were standing on. There had been other owners in between them and him. But he didn't know anything about the Saitos.

We got permission to drive up to the house and look around. The silver poplars were still there, looking a bit sad, it seemed to me. The house had not been used as a house for many years. When I looked in the window, all I could make out were some old white kitchen cabinets on the floor and one hanging askew on the wall. Those cabinets, so popular at that time, were made of metal and painted white. They were lightweight and held up like any other piece of solid farm equipment. I've never seen metal kitchen cabinets since leaving my grandparents' home. Grandpa's lush gardens were gone, and the house and a couple of outbuildings were now surrounded by fields of sugar beets and wheat, the crops Dad had grown and still the main farm crops in that area. After a short walk around what was left of the yard, we got in the car and headed back to the highway. I needed to make one other stop.

My former schoolhouse, set back a short distance from the highway but easily seen, was also still standing. It looked even smaller than I had remembered, but it didn't look shabby or rundown. The paint, while not brand new, was new enough to make the school look used and cared for. There was a car or two in the yard and play equipment on the grounds. As Jan and I ventured toward the entrance, we noticed several little kids, barely older than toddlers, playing in the yard. We reached the door and peeked in. The single room was filled with little children. My old country schoolhouse of grades one through six and at one time grades one through eight was now an active pre-school! It made me feel happy to see the room filled with light, with colorful toys and objects, humming with life and activity and the sound of shrill little voices piercing the air. I realized in that moment how I had dreaded finding another rundown building filled with dust and discarded objects, in this case old-fashioned desks, chalkboards scratched and falling off walls, and no signs of life having been there in years. What a relief to see little ones filling the space. Jan and I had another courteous conversation with one of the teachers who recognized a name or two but couldn't give us much information about the old-timers in the area. Not wanting to interrupt his day any more than we already had, we left and drove slowly back toward town. We would stay the night, explore the town the next day—which might take a full fifteen minutes—and move on.

I could almost swear that Hardin was smaller, with even fewer stores, than it had been when I was growing up there. Or maybe it was just that I was grown up and now seeing everything from an adult perspective. But I think not. I think the town itself had been through hard times that had left their mark. There had been two clothing stores on Main Street that I could think of, and as far as we knew in those days, both kept up with the fashion trends of the time; but both had disappeared and nothing similar had taken their places. The Western store, which had sold things like saddles and Western-style cowboy shirts and cowboy boots, was also gone. The family that had run it had been friends of ours, especially their daughter who was a friend of Lilian's. Had they moved on? And to where? Now there were a few shops with unfamiliar names selling things—clothing, standard drugstore fare—that one could find just about anywhere, but there was not much available. No, Main Street definitely seemed slightly worse for wear than it had been when I was a kid going into town with Mom to do our shopping.

The Safeway was still there; I remembered hearing that one had moved to Hardin shortly after we left. It was a big supermarket, and its arrival had been a big deal for a small town. Now it was also showing its age, not looking bright and shiny like one-stop urban Safeways tend to look. We went inside to look around and get some junk food to snack on, and at the checkout (no line) I told the cashier, a young white man who looked like an older adolescent, that I had once lived in the area. He was totally unimpressed. Had nothing to ask me or tell me.

In many Asian cultures it is traditional to visit the graves of ancestors at regular intervals, perhaps on some national day set aside for such duties or perhaps at times established by family members. Even though my siblings and I are third-generation Japanese Americans, we have tried to maintain some Old World traditions, but most of them have become pretty shabby and frayed, sporadic at best. My decision to go to the Hardin cemetery to try to find my grandparents' graves was driven in part by a guilty conscience for not ever having made the effort to visit in the past and, at this late date, to finally pay some respect to their memories, if not their headstones. The other reason for going was simple curiosity: Who else from my childhood days would I find resting there? Who from my parents' generation that I had spent time with, playing with their kids, eating their cookies, and drinking their Kool-Aid? Who might be left alive to visit?

We found the headstones for Grandpa and Grandma, simple with names and dates and surrounded by green, clipped grass. I was struck and saddened by how small a tribute it was to two lives that loomed so large in my memory. I was grateful that someone was maintaining the cemetery overall. Everything was green and trimmed and, as to be expected, some gravestones were better kept up than others. Some looked as though they had been visited fairly recently, since fresh flowers had been placed in small vases or laid in front of the headstones. Another relief, since what could be more depressing than a forgotten cemetery overgrown with weeds and sagebrush.

I dragged Jan through rows of other gravestones with Japanese names, searching for ones I recognized. Jan was no help, of course, not just because he had trouble pronouncing the names but because he had no idea what names to look for; in a way, I didn't really either. I knew a few family surnames and could remember a few of the first names of the moms and dads, but the first names of some of the elders were mysteries since we kids grew up calling the eldest generation Mr. and Mrs. Our quick walk-through seemed to be telling us that many adults of my parents' generation were still alive, as were my parents at that time, though they would be gone in a few short years. They formed an elderly group, so it felt gratifying to find so few of their names engraved on the stones.

Somewhere in a pile of unlabeled pictures, I have a snapshot of three people sitting beside Jan and me. We appear to be in a café, since there are partially filled water glasses and a few empty dishes on the table. It looks like a casual place, since the table could be Formica or plastic encased with a narrow metal band and there is no tablecloth. The three people are elderly but smiling and not unhealthy-looking. They are three of the remaining Japanese American farmers Jan and I were able to track down and spontaneously invite to a get-together. Three parents from my childhood who were gracious enough to meet with us after never having heard a word from me after we left the area, not even a yearly Christmas card. I am having trouble remembering what we talked about, since that meeting took place nearly twenty years ago and the time between then and when I'd first known them was nearly double that. Where does one even begin? We probably talked about what their children—most a few years younger than me but still middle-aged adults—were doing and where they were living, whom they had married, and how many grandchildren the present company could boast of. Even though I was physically present at the table, there is a big gap in my memory, as if someone else were telling me their experience. I can't explain it; why the big gap about something I personally experienced as an adult, indeed, as someone who had sought out the occasion? All I can come up with is that it was overwhelming. Far too much time, history, life, and lives had taken place between my childhood and that moment.

In fact, it was not really a gap but a large expanse filled to the brim with everything one can imagine, all of life's vagaries, and it would have taken a lot of time, patience, caring, and goodwill to sort through all of it. In retrospect, when I think of that picture, I would now say that it was probably a mistake to have gotten together, to have asked for such a meeting. I am sure I didn't insult or act like a dolt toward these old family friends, but I didn't take advantage of a rich opportunity to really find out about them or their lives. In my state of overwhelm, I kept the conversation light and superficial, and in the end the gap was filled with fluff.

Today, that trip is nearly ancient history. More people from my childhood have passed on, including my parents and some of my aunts and uncles. I have never made another visit to Montana and should I decide to take one, it wouldn't be to see Hardin but to enjoy the mountains and natural beauty of the western part of the state. The part we didn't live in.

I rarely talk about my Montana life with anyone, and I only do so if I am asked directly about where I was born, where I grew up, where I went to grade school, or some other question that necessitates my going that far back in my history. I think it has been mostly shame that has stopped me, the shame about growing up in an area of the country so seemingly remote that people rarely thought about it and automatically thought everyone from there was a hayseed. Even more powerful was the added shame of rural poverty. And then, of course, we were not only rural, and poor, but we weren't white. What a perfect combination for keeping mute about one's past or at least one's childhood. But it was a bad cycle: when I got old enough to realize my feelings of shame, I felt guilty for feeling ashamed. But not guilty enough to want to talk about growing up in Montana.

I was lucky that I found psychology and, through my work, made it an everyday part of my life. Otherwise, I might never have come to understand the concept of trauma and how it is experienced. Of course, as I have been saying all along, the number one rule pertaining to trauma is not to talk about it. So in my family, we never did. We kids never heard our parents or grandparents discuss the war, the forced removal, the prejudice and racism they and their friends faced during and after that time. My parents' trauma of forced removal, loss, displacement, and finally relocation became a story that had to unfold in surprising and upsetting clumps throughout my life. But now I understand that if trauma unfolds at all, that's the way it usually happens.

One afternoon in 2012, completely inadvertently, I encountered a graphic and disturbing example of this ragged unfolding of trauma. I had decided to escape to the movies, something I had especially loved doing on weekend afternoons when I was still working full-time and needed a break before beginning a new work week. The fun of it was not only that I love movies but that I treasured the feeling of sneaking out by myself and heading to a dark cave where no one would likely see or recognize me and I could be thoroughly entertained without saying a word or lifting a finger. Even though by the time in question I was officially retired, I still loved spontaneously dropping everything and heading off to the movies on my own. It was almost sweeter now that I could go anytime—I didn't have to wait until the weekend. The movie that afternoon was *The Flat*, a documentary by an Israeli filmmaker, Arnon Goldfinger. Beyond that I knew nothing about it except that from the short descriptive blurb, it sounded like a good story might be lurking there.

It turned out that *The Flat* set off a short chain reaction in my brain. The story itself was compelling, certainly one of a kind, but the message I took from it was a validation of all I believed and understood about the effects of trauma. I could see the skeleton of my parents' story and my own in its tale of a Jewish family, the Tuchlers. The movie was filmed in Tel Aviv, where the filmmaker's family had lived for many years. Goldfinger's maternal grandmother, Gerda Tuchler, had died at ninety-eight, and he and several cousins had gone to her flat to do the tedious job of cleaning it out. Gerda's husband, Kurt, who had died some years earlier, had been a judge, and they appeared to have lived a solid middle-class life.

At first, the clearing-out process goes as many such projects do—the apartment, or flat, is filled to the brim with things held on to for decades: drawers and closets full of gloves, handbags, shoes, jewelry, and clothing—including a fox-fur piece, head and tail still intact, which is passed from cousin to cousin to inspect, try on, and laugh at. There are shelves of books, many of the classics of literature, all in German. Other drawers are full of all kinds of documents, including old newspaper clippings. Their grandmother, it seems, saved everything. Arnon's mother, Hannah, would like to make a clean sweep and get rid of things, but Arnon wants to go through the papers—the documents and newspaper clippings—to find out what new things he can of his grandparents' life. What he discovers is the meat of the movie: Arnon learns that his grandparents were very good lifelong friends with a man named Leopold von Mildenstein and his wife. Mildenstein was head of the Nazi SS Office for Jewish Affairs prior to Adolf Eichmann taking it over; in fact, Mildenstein recruited and hired Eichmann for the job. I use the words *lifelong friendship* because the friendship between the Tuchlers and the Mildensteins continued unbroken throughout the duration of World War II and afterward. It was at the suggestion of the Mildensteins that the Tuchers had immigrated to Palestine in the 1930s.

Needless to say, Arnon is more than shocked to learn about this relationship between his beloved grandparents and a Nazi murderer, someone who was most likely responsible for the deaths not only of family friends but also of some family members. As the filmmaker, he courageously shows himself digging deep into this unwelcome chapter of his family's history. He interviews his mother, trying to ascertain what she knew about the Nazi couple and what she remembers about her parents' relationship with them. It appears that Hannah didn't know what von Mildenstein did for a living, and when she is told point blank, the shock for the audience is that she seems not to be surprised or much disturbed by the information. Her bland response astonishes and confounds Arnon, and he tries to probe her for a more emotionally real response. His own emotional restraint and objective reporting are admirable. Hannah, however, remains impassive throughout the film. She does not want to discuss the past; she wants to leave the past alone. One reviewer of the film describes her "continued refusal to be moved by his revelations" as "willful amnesia." By the end of the film, Hannah has shifted very little, remaining emotionally removed from the terrible truth of her parents' mysterious friendship with a couple who themselves may have been crossing into improbable territory by maintaining their friendship with Jews, people the SS officer was in charge of exterminating in other countries.

Arnon Goldfinger had encountered a gap in his grandparents' history that he didn't know existed, and when he discovered it and went to fill in the details, he uncovered a horrifying and almost unbelievable story—one he had more than a little trouble comprehending, interpreting, and integrating into his own narrative of his family history and of history itself.

I admit my own ignorance about how to truly understand the friendship of the Tuchlers and the Mildensteins throughout the time the Nazi genocide of the Jews was in full operation. I can only assume that trauma played a part in the story because I know how trauma can keep any story from being discussed or even mentioned. I know that victims of trauma try very hard to carry on as if nothing bad has happened to them or to a close loved one. So the Tuchlers had carried on with their lives as normally as possible—raising a family, having the social life suitable for a judge and his wife, and from the looks of their books and pictures, enjoying an active intellectual life. Everything else, including the friendship that had probably saved their lives, went into the gap.

I can relate to Arnon's surprise and shock at discovering this very hidden chapter of his grandparents' life. One film critic professes that the real subject of *The Flat* is the "generational divide." The generation directly experiencing the trauma, like Hannah, would prefer to leave the past alone. They think to themselves, "It is over, so why dig it up?" But thankfully, the generations that follow—Arnon and in my family myself, my siblings, and their children—want to know about our families, to learn about our histories. For Americans, that's probably in part because we know that the founding of the United States is fairly recent history and that everyone who isn't an American Indian came here from somewhere else. When, from where, how, and why did all these people come? We are curious, we want to know about grandparents or our great-grandparents or our parents. We want to find out before too much time has passed and information is lost when our elders start to die. So we take the risk and dive in—into the gap.

Finding out about our past can explain parts of our lives we never understood before. Something as simple as why my brother-in-law can't stand the sight of a banana because they used to get truckloads of black, overripe bananas to eat in Topaz Internment Camp, where he and his family were imprisoned during the war. Or something as powerful as why my father was never able to finish his college education and pursue the profession he wanted—an engineer or a dentist—because his life was thrust onto a completely different trajectory when he, his wife, and daughter had to go to a farm in Wyoming to avoid being placed in an incarceration camp. Gaps small and large that illuminate when filled in.

4

Big Apple to Big Sky

Meditations on Space

I should have taken a picture as proof of the trip and of that memory so fixed in my mind. But I was caught off-guard—I didn't have my camera. My friend Margot and I had decided, in a spontaneous moment of abandon, to make a spur-of-the-moment trip from her Boston home to New York City. We would have only a few dizzying hours there before I was scheduled to go home to Berkeley. On our short list was a much anticipated whirlwind visit to the High Line, the old elevated railroad track refashioned into a park, its first section opened to the public in 2009.

Our tight schedule allowed us just a brief stroll along a short distance of the walkway. The workday was winding down; it was summer and daylight had not yet begun to shrink. As we stood there, looking up at the empty open sky and down upon the city below, booming with life, the calming spirit of the park took over; and we felt our very mature bodies, stiff from travel, relax. I fell in love with that park and could have stayed forever.

The High Line struck me then and even more so now as an ingenious, functional, and beautiful way to make use of an old, tired, no longer in service railroad track that once ran through the heart of New York City's west side: the meatpacking district, West Chelsea, and Hell's Kitchen. In the early 1900s, the track was still at street level, and the west side was home to over 250 slaughterhouses and meatpacking plants that processed the raw materials. Having the railroad right there made it easy to get goods in and out.

But it was dangerous for people to walk in the area. Pedestrians were sometimes killed or injured trying to avoid the traffic. Standing in this beautiful park high above the street, I imagined that time. I could see myself down there, on the alert as I pick my way through those streets, dodging carts, trucks, and trains, stepping gingerly around pools of blood and other unidentifiable animal body fluids. I try not to take deep breaths because what makes me recoil most are the imagined smells. The overbearing odors of raw meat and blood and the contents of guts permeating the air, especially in the heat of a New York City summer, soaking deep into the pores of the workers so that nothing, not even showers with strong soap and hot water, could fully eliminate the smell. It was the smell of death as much as that of life and livelihood and food. And what about the sounds? Were passersby barraged by the squeals and moans of animals at the slaughter even above the sound of traffic? It must have been deafening. Up here it was almost silent by contrast, and I wondered how many workers did go deaf.

I don't know who came up with the bold idea to elevate the track, but in 1930, freight traffic was majestically lifted thirty feet into the air. The streets were opened to the free flow of pedestrians and pedestrian-friendly traffic, and the trains could roll directly onto the upper floors of the packing houses and manufacturing buildings to load and unload their goods. The accident rate dropped. It was all good—until it wasn't.

The automobile was what finally killed the High Line. The booming auto industry, combined with a freeway system that connected the country, made trucking the way to move goods quickly and efficiently. So despite its struggle to hold on, in 1980, according to its official website, the last train ran on the High Line "pulling three cars of frozen turkeys." It seemed to me a sad, undignified demise for a once-powerful engine of industry.

The track, useless and neglected, started to erode and become an eyesore. There was talk of demolishing it. Fortunately, in 1999, some locals with heart, drive, and connections came together, saved the track, and—with a great deal of vision and hard work—transformed it into a public space for all New

Yorkers to use and enjoy. The new High Line park gained a reputation as a place to visit, so tourists now flock there. Having been one of those tourists and having my own prejudices about recycling, I think it was a terrific idea.

In spite of its unusual height, this park is like most others: it is fully land-scaped for maximum public pleasure. In addition to narrow stretches that are perfect for leisurely strolling, there are also generous open spaces to allow musicians to play everything from rock guitar to cello; performers to perform plays, magic shows, stand-up comedy; children to play running games with friends and parents. In our short stroll, Margot and I saw people of all ages sitting on the benches and reading, eating takeout or drinking coffee, or engaged in focused conversation. There was greenery everywhere. Some of the trees, bushes, and grasses are the same plants that were there before the track was refurbished and transformed because the landscapers had the wisdom to incorporate them and not consider them throwaways, not manicured enough for a new park.

The park is a treasure for the city of New York, but for me, the real magic of the place is that it is thirty feet in the air. This thirty-foot height seems like the ideal elevation for both looking up and looking down: it's an aerial view of the sky—which from up there seems vaster, closer, more enveloping—and of the city, spread out below where everything is smaller but the people still look like people. As we view them, we remain a part of them; they are not ants in a fast-forward march to some place they never reach. At this perfect elevation, the spirit, free and untethered, floats upward but the body stays earthbound, keeping us unquestionably human.

Reluctant to depart but needing to move on, Margot and I found one of the elevators located handily along the length of the park. With a quick ride down, we once again became anonymous in the crowd on the street.

• • •

In eastern Montana, no matter what land formations surround you or what river runs through your town or pasture, the sky is the same for everyone. And that would be big. Very big. Huge, spacious, overarching. Sometimes dazzlingly clear and blue, at other times filled with clouds—puffy, marshmallowy cumulus; dark and stormy nimbus; or feathery cirrus, all giving hints of the weather to one who knows how to read them. At night, the Milky Way, undiminished by the glow of city lights, stands out like a clear path to infinity.

The land beneath this vast sky is mostly flat and dry; the summers have spells of searing heat, the winters of bitter cold, and the winds can come at any time. In the summers of my childhood, from early morning through the hottest part of the day, housewives kept the curtains drawn and blinds closed to stave off the heat for as long as possible, making each ordinary house look like a place in mourning with the kids trapped inside, bored, listless, and mournful. In winter, the snow can drift over roads and animals and low buildings, making it hard for people to get to grocery stores or to their barns and sheds or to take care of their livestock. I've seen old pictures of my siblings and me in a snowball fight on top of drifts covering the roof of the toolshed.

When spring came to our farm, it brought the snowmelt from the Rockies in the west, filling the Bighorn and the other rivers enough to irrigate the crops. Those irrigated deep-green beet tops and nearly translucent green blades of wheat stood out in sharp contrast against the mostly yellow of the drying plains of summer. My sisters and I frequently played around the little streams of water flowing through our pastureland, a kind of seepage from the larger rivers. Sometimes, if we were lucky, we saw a great blue heron hunting in the water, and one time we saw it take off, its huge wings lifting it gracefully into the air. In the winter our dad took us to a wooded area where that seepage had frozen over and we could ice skate on it. Gliding fast over the ice made me feel light and unencumbered, as though I, too, could take flight if I could work up enough speed and get rid of my heavy jacket.

But those wide-open plains were not without perils. Much later in life, when I was an adult living in a city, I heard about a man who had been killed by a lightning strike somewhere on the plains of Ohio, and I was instantly flooded with vivid memories and images of our Montana lightning storms. As a child, I had it backward: it was the thunder, that loud cracking sound, that splitting of the air followed by a rolling boom, that scared me most. That was before I learned that the lightning that caused the sound was really the thing to be afraid of. My sisters and I could be playing in an open field or our garden and the sky would begin to darken; the clouds would change from rolling cumulus into dark nimbus—thunderclouds heavy with rain. And then there would be the lightning, that jagged, golden stem of heat and electricity, beginning way up high, materializing out of nothing but sky, thrown earthward: a stunning flash in a rapidly darkening world. Usually, that serrated streak would head in a straight line directly toward the ground. But sometimes it would fool us and shoot out horizontally in crooked, branching lines to disappear, literally, into thin air. We couldn't help but stop what we were doing to watch the light show. And then the rain would come, sometimes in big, splattering drops, and everyone who happened to be outside at the time would head for the nearest shelter—a house, a shed or barn, or sometimes a tree. Now I know that a tree is not a safe place to seek cover in an electrical storm because it can draw the lightning to you. But we didn't know that as kids dashing across the open plain trying to outrun a thunderstorm.

But the storms, as dramatic as they were, are not what I remember most of the Montana sky. It's the way the sky made everything else look, how the line of the horizon stretched out forever, well beyond my child's imagination. When we looked at something distant, it was next to impossible to tell how far or close we were to it; a land formation—a butte or some hilly mounds—took on its defining shape only when we shortened the distance between it and ourselves. The sky simply took over. It dominated. The ratio of land to sky at any given time was the perfect ratio for a painting or a photograph: one third to two thirds, we are taught, to energize the picture. The plains and sky of Montana were naturally primed for the perfect picture.

Konrad Lorenz, an Austrian scientist, conducted an experiment that gave him a place in popular science. He made himself, instead of the mother goose, the first thing seen by a small gaggle of hatchling geese. The result was that he imprinted himself on their brains, and they took him for their mother. They followed him everywhere, just as they would their mother. As a child waking up each morning to the Montana sky, the same thing happened to me: I was imprinted with that sky. Whenever I go to a movie that shows a broad, roomy expanse of plain, desert, steppe, or meadow, I am immediately mesmerized. I am filled with a sense of wonder as well as a kind of well-being, as if that capaciousness has infiltrated my very insides and surrounded my organs with pockets of air, making me taller. Giving me hope. It is the same with still photos I come across: a monk walking along the spare Tibetan tundra, a sweep of gold or green Midwest farm country, Mongols playing polo on smallish ponies kicking up the dust of a wide, dry plain. In each photo frame, in each movie scene, it's the sky that makes the land. A sky so huge that it doesn't matter what else is in the picture, it can still look almost empty. The people and animals are fascinating, but it's that emptiness they are trying to fill that arrests my gaze, makes me linger over the photo, drives my curiosity to know where they are even more than who they are. Lorenz became fused to the geese: the vast Montana sky remains embedded in me.

My enthusiasm for "big sky country" may make it seem like I was sad to leave it, sad to leave farming and country life. The opposite is true: a big part of me wanted to get away from Montana. I knew Dad was struggling to run the farm by himself.

Having three young daughters and a toddler son does not bode well for a future in farming. Before Dad was born, he had lost a sister, making him an only child. He had no reliable male to help him with the myriad tasks required to run a farm. Most of the Japanese American farmers we knew in our valley came from big families: fathers and sons, brothers, and brothers-in-law who stuck together and worked their farms as a team. It made everything easier and more affordable when both labor and the ever more expensive farm equipment could be shared. And their social needs were more simply met because, when time allowed, the men had each other to drink and play cards with. The same was true for their wives and, eventually, their children. The cousins could play with each other, and one of the mothers or aunties could be found to baby-sit while the others went to buy groceries, go to the doctor or dentist, or run errands. In a crisis, all the families came together, pooled their resources—financial, social, and emotional—and took care of the problem. A collective family spirit made the entire endeavor a shared experience—the failures, the successes, and the demands of everyday life. For these families, in the long run, farming actually paid off.

Dad, in contrast, had to take care of everything himself. He became my version of the Renaissance man; he could, I knew, do everything. You could find him on his back underneath a truck making repairs or chatting with our county agent, a large, soft-spoken man with granny glasses who told him about new plant varieties, farming techniques, and what to read to learn more. He took care of the livestock and learned how to take care of ailing pigs, cows, or sheep—and when to call the veterinarian when he had run out of options. Mom also had to go it alone, figuring out how to raise four small children by herself. I can't remember how she managed this, but I don't remember ever feeling neglected in any way. My siblings and I could entertain each other from an early age, but we weren't that helpful with farm work.

As I got older and especially as I headed into my teens, I could tell that the pressures of running a farm single-handedly were taking their toll on my parents. I could see it in the worry behind their eyes, the sag of their faces by nightfall, and the way Dad shook his head when the subject of crops came up. Looking back, I marvel at the memories I have of Dad reading to us when we were very young. I don't know where he found the energy.

I was a year into junior high when Dad finally decided it was time to quit farming—he couldn't keep up with the accumulating debt—and move back to the city. I was delighted when I learned that we were moving to Denver, a true big city, even bigger than Billings. There was no question that I would miss our grandparents, especially my grandmother, who had always done everything she could to make our farm life richer. But in Denver, I thought, we would have so much more—even cousins close to our ages thrown into the mix. In my excitement, I didn't stop to think that Grandma and Grandpa would miss us, their only grandchildren.

I always liked going to school, but I was also glad to be leaving my one-room country schoolhouse. I knew I would be genuinely sad to leave Beverly, my best friend, but my feelings of loss were balanced by the sheer excitement I felt thinking about being in a big-city school where there would be lots of kids my age. I would have more than one good girlfriend because there would be lots of girls to choose from. I would go to movies and parties and encounter other things I couldn't yet imagine. Leaving the farm would mean, I thought, leaving behind that feeling of aloneness and isolation that had surrounded me and my entire family for so long. Going to a city would mean being surrounded by hundreds of people, mostly ones I didn't know and never would, as well as by buildings and houses as far as the eye could see. It would mean mystery and romance of every kind. I was a budding adolescent, and I was ready for more—more people, more girlfriends, more things to do. I was ready for a change.

My romance with cities had most likely begun with our family trips to Billings, one of the larger towns in Montana. Billings was located in the foothills of the Rockies about fifty miles west of Hardin, the very small town closest to us. In limited little Hardin, if we couldn't find what we were looking for or if something didn't fit, we were out of luck. We couldn't make the trip often, but if we needed to do any serious shopping, we would have to leave the flatlands of our farm and drive to Billings. As we wound around curves on our gradual ascent into the city, we watched the vegetation and landscape change from yellow grasses and weeds to cottonwood and poplar to pine forests carpeting the ascending hills. I remember more than once making Dad stop the car by the side of the road so I could get out, throw up if I needed to, and switch to the front seat.

Chancing the carsickness was worth it. I loved going to Billings because a trip to the city was an excursion, an event. My sisters and I could barely keep from tripping as we walked down the sidewalk, looking up with wonder at the tall buildings and the fancy signs announcing the names of businesses and goods; we would gaze in the store windows with their mannequins decked out in the latest fashions and wonder who wore clothes like that and where they went; we would stop at our favorite bakery for the maple bars we had been craving from the moment we got to the outskirts of town. There were two department stores we would always go to, and no matter how often we went we would stare, mouths open, at the entire floor of clothing for kids. In the fancier store, my sisters and I would beg to spend at least a few minutes, even if we couldn't afford to buy anything, watching the canisters speed through the pneumatic tubes that crisscrossed the ceiling, each one delivering some mysterious message to another department in the store. We watched wide-eyed with delight and anticipation as a clerk opened the end of the tube and inserted a canister that was then sucked up with a swooshing sound and shot through the tubing. We would follow it with our eyes, heads tilted back, and listen for the dull thump at the other end where another clerk would take it out and retrieve the message, something so important that it had to be conveyed right then and there. That was the only place I had ever witnessed this magical delivery system, only one of the delights that awaited us, I was sure, in our new big city.

And as it turned out, I love living in a city. Urban life has suited me, and I have never abandoned it. I have taken to all the ways it has invaded the isolation of my childhood and stimulated my mind and my senses. I love the tight, compact connection with humanity; the way it feels when we jostle each other on crowded sidewalks and without intention bump into each other in supermarkets and malls; when we sit elbow to elbow with each other at the movies, eat next to each other in restaurants, drink together in favorite bars and cafés. And when we dress up and go to the opera, the symphony, the theater. Sometimes we look into each other's faces, sometimes we avert our eyes. No matter if we are strangers or longtime friends, we are communing together in a shared urban experience, partaking of the riches, doing our best to cope with the annoyances. We challenge each other and inspire each other just by being in the same airspace. Sometimes it seems as if we exchange molecules, but maybe that happens only between loved ones.

• • •

As I stood on the High Line in New York City that waning afternoon, my childhood memories of Montana and the Montana sky came flooding back to me. I was caught off guard, completely unprepared for that memory to arrive there. But holding onto the railing of the fence and looking up, I saw a sky that was vast, open, endless—and the freedom and innocence of my childhood under that other huge sky awakened within me, filling me with wonder and calm and long-forgotten images of the past. Yet looking down, I saw the vitality of big-city life, and I became part of it too, of the undulating drone of hundreds of voices filling the air; of cars, the hum of their motors punctuated by the sharp honking of horns, forming a kind of chaotic rhythm; of the steady, staccato beat of shoes landing hard on pavement; of the pulsing flow of crowds of people stopping at corners as one body, then surging forward together like the crest of a wave; of the high-octane energy of everything in constant motion.

It turns out that I didn't need my camera after all because the pictures are there, fixed in my memory. Pictures I can call up anytime to remind me of that magical spot where past and present, time and space, rural and urban came together as one, and in that elusive moment, so did my life.

5

THE ONE AND ONLY

I'm not sure why I never framed them and hung them on my wall, not on any wall, not in my office or anywhere in my home. That's usually what people do with their diplomas or certificates, the proof of their achievements. Perhaps it goes back to that standard Japanese cultural practice of not doing anything that smacks even a little bit of showing off. I saw degrees and certifications on the walls of every therapy office I ever entered, but it took me awhile to compute the fact that I, too, had degrees and certifications that I could hang on my office walls. I had a diploma showing I had a master's degree in clinical social work; I had a license in that field issued from the state of California, acquired only after passing an exam; I had a diploma from my professional organization showing a certain number of years of membership and a higher level of clinical achievement, and I had my bachelor's degree in English. All tucked away in my trusty file cabinet. The only things on my office walls were the other person's certifications and degrees—since I usually shared my office with another therapist—and a picture or two, reproductions of some famous person's artwork.

It wasn't that I didn't take pride in those totems of success. I was the first in my family to go beyond a bachelor's degree, and I was proud of that. I was proud of passing my licensing exam and obtaining my California license to practice. But after mastering those hurdles, it seemed there were always other hurdles ahead. And there was always the work itself to be done. Work unlike any other, so it seemed. Work requiring both mind and heart, distance and closeness, objectivity and intimacy. Work that allowed one party, the therapist, to learn the most intimate details in the life of the person who had come seeking help and at the same time to reveal next to nothing about herself. How does one become intimate with, form a trusting relationship with, someone who doesn't share the experience of her life while the person across from her is revealing usually painful, long-held secrets?

But such is the work of therapy.

When I was trying to decide on a career, I barely knew what it meant to be a psychotherapist—the word itself sounded a little pretentious, with its many syllables, or maybe even a little suspect. I mean, anything starting with the word *psycho* in today's popular culture can carry frightening connotations. I knew I wanted to do something professional, to *find* a profession, but psychotherapy was an unlikely, if not downright strange, choice for an Asian American, especially in the early 1970s.

I had been employed steadily since graduating from college in the mid-1960s, but nothing was developing into a real "career." When I'd graduated with a bachelor's degree in English, I had also armed myself with a teaching credential, since that was the only thing I could think to do with an otherwise impractical degree. But student teaching had not gone well for me. Once, when my master teacher was observing my classroom, I noticed that about halfway through the lesson he put his head down on his desk. I was waiting to hear him snore to make the humiliation complete! Relating to so many people at one time, trying to make information interesting for them, trying to maintain discipline in the room, trying to stay human and remember that the students were also human—no, that was way too much for me to handle all at once. There had to be some other way to earn a living while also holding onto my staunch belief that I had to do something of worth in this world, in this lifetime.

Back when I was a teenager, I became aware of a pervasive stereotype about Asian American students and Asian Americans in general: that they are the "model minority." A model minority is perceived as just that: a model of better-than-average achievement and success in almost every way—educationally, economically, socially. Asian American families, the story went, were more stable, the parents made more money, and overall they were better educated than the average middle-class American. They were happy and friendly, worked hard, never got into or caused trouble, and, in truth, were barely noticed.

Furthermore, everyone assumed that their children, Asian American students, excelled in math and the sciences and went on to become scientists, engineers, nurses, and doctors. After graduation, they easily found jobs and propagated the model.

As with any stereotype, there is a grain of truth here that everything else is wrapped around and grossly exaggerates. In the case of Asian American students, I knew why the stereotype included the nerd with the briefcase and slide rule (at least before the days of laptop computers) scurrying off to math and science classes. The sciences are more practical than other fields, and it is true that the prospects of getting a job after graduation—high on the priority list for Asian parents—are better by far if you have a degree in a science rather than in something like, well, English or history.

The other advantage the sciences hold over the humanities for Asian American students is that most fields of science have their own scientific language—Latin categories, mathematical terms and equations, universal names of all matter of things living and long gone. Anyone who learns science also learns that language and can communicate both in speaking and writing with another scientist in the office next door or on the other side of the country. A portion of Asian American students grow up with parents who are bilingual but less fluent in English than in their mother tongue or, in some cases, are monolingual. Sometimes, households are multigenerational, with the older adults non-English speakers. It isn't unusual for kids growing up in such a household to be bilingual themselves, or at least they are able to understand the other language and know enough to communicate with the adults at home. These kids learn to speak what sounds like perfect English—but understanding the structure of the language and writing it coherently and precisely is a different story. Writing becomes an invisible handicap. A hidden defect. A struggle to be avoided if at all possible. If you have any issues with English, studying science, with its own built-in language, makes a lot more sense. So just as I had steered away from math and science classes when I was in college, many Asian American students among my peers continued to find English and history classes difficult to maneuver without a lot of extra guidance.

In our family, it was the kids who were monolingual: English was our first and only language. In Montana, our little one-room country schoolhouse had, besides us, only white students who spoke only English. After leaving our farm for good and moving to Denver, we went to all-white schools, interacted daily with white students and teachers, and came home to an all-white neighborhood. We grew up hearing, reading, thinking, and writing in English. My Japanese was probably the same as that of anyone else who had bothered to learn to say hello, thank you, and sayonara in Japanese—so it did not seem strange that when I went on to college I ended up making English my major at CU, the University of Colorado in Boulder. I had always liked literature, and I'd never found the grammar or syntax of writing term papers a problem. I did pretty well with organizing my thoughts for an essay test. And I knew myself well enough to stay away from the mysterious math and science classes. So in almost all my classes—literature, grammar, and philosophy—I was the standout student, in skin shade only. I rarely encountered another Asian student in courses for my English major. It wasn't always comfortable—I always checked to see if I could find another Asian face—but basically, I had become inured to being the only Asian pretty much everywhere I went.

Certainly, there were other Asian students on campus and I would see them, often in clusters of twos and threes, but it remained a puzzle to me as to how to get to know them, how to get their attention or find an opportunity to speak with them. Occasionally, something would come up to make this happen. In my sophomore year there was a Japanese American woman who lived in my dorm. We did manage to find each other and spent time hanging out together. But there was something wrong about it, and mostly it was me: I didn't quite fit in. Something was missing in my ability to connect. As I got to know her better, I realized we had shared little in common in our lives before coming to CU. She had grown up in a tight Denver Japanese American community and had lots of friends there. Some of them were at CU, and sometimes I would join her when she did things with them on campus. But I was always the outlier, the one who didn't quite know the social references or the names or the events, past and future, that everyone else seemed completely familiar with. They all seemed to have some past life in common. It didn't take me long to figure out that that life was either at the church or at their schools, maybe as far back as junior high. Even more bonding and binding for all of them, and what I conspicuously lacked, was the near-universal Japanese American experience of having families who had spent around three years of their lives during World War II incarcerated in an American concentration camp. Finally, I was neither a Methodist nor a Buddhist, the two religious gathering places for Japanese Americans in Denver, and, as I've mentioned, at my schools I had always been the only Asian student.

The school year ended and we went home for the summer break, and when I returned in the fall, I rarely saw this woman. Eventually, we lost touch altogether.

I can honestly say that I never adjusted to college life. I rarely enjoyed being there, and academically I was a sorry example of the stellar Asian student. In fact, while I didn't fail any classes, I was always stressed out about exams or even about being called on in class because I was typically ill prepared. My study habits were deplorable, and I was consistently behind in the piles of reading required of English majors. Exam times were a nightmare, and today it is horrifying to think back on all the exams I took without having finished the reading. Up until just a few years ago, I would have a recurring, telltale dream at least twice a year: I was in college and it was final exam time. I was in my room trying to study, but I was in a complete panic because I had not read any of the required books, and they were all there, everywhere, surrounding me in tall piles, some brand-new, their spines uncracked. I would never catch up. I would fail the class. How would I explain this to my parents? The dream scenario was exaggerated, to be sure, but it contained the kernel of terrifying truth: in college I was behind in everything, and if I wanted to pass my classes, I always had a ton of catching up to do. Sometimes in the dream I would hope, actually pray, "please, dear God, let this be a dream," and then I would wake up with a start, look around, and sigh in huge relief. For many, many years, the dream would pop up right around the time of final exams, just before the school semester was coming to a close. It seemed like muscle memory: a version of something that had happened to me so often that I could remember it without even consciously thinking about it.

My unconscious memory, right on cue, would dredge up this old anxiety, in this very vivid form, and remind me what time of year it was.

Of course, college is a time for big ideas and when I was in college in the 1960s, big social ideas were dominating the scene. It was the time of a landmark civil rights struggle in the nation, at times violent and bloody; the war in Vietnam was raging and splitting the country into a group of angry bodies protesting against it and a group of equally angry bodies protesting against the protestors. A small number of students were starting to slip over the border into Canada to avoid being drafted to fight a war they couldn't understand or morally support. Some places—some campuses—were experiencing violence among students, between students and the police, and between students and their administrations; at the University of California, Berkeley, the students were having a passionate standoff with the administration, the now famous Free Speech Movement. College campuses across the United States were in turmoil, and my campus was having its share of unrest. I mean, how does any college student ignore a war and a seminal struggle for long-overdue justice?

For me, it turned out to be just too much, too much of everything. Too many big ideas, too many students on campus, too many classes to choose from, too much academically to keep on top of, too much excitement generated by the world beyond the ivory towers. How to focus on the things that were in front of me and not get pulled off center by a half dozen others that seemed important or interesting or something college students should be participating in? How to sort out what was really important to me and let everything else go? I liken my time at CU to being in a restaurant. During that time in my life, I could be in a restaurant with a friend, having a pleasant conversation. At some point it wouldn't be unusual for me to say to my companion, "Did you hear that—what that person at that table over there," my eyes rolling right or left, "just said?" On rare occasions, my companion would know exactly what I was referring to, but usually she would be either surprised or displeased, thinking I had not been paying attention to her or to our conversation. But that wasn't true: I was listening to my friend, but without meaning to, I could also hear enough of the other table's conversation to know what was going on. I wasn't rude enough to interject myself into the other conversation, but I also couldn't shut it out completely. Being on a college campus was the same: I couldn't shut out all that other activity around me, and the distraction kept me from being a dedicated student. Everything and everyone seemed important. I was constantly being pulled in too many different directions at once. I had trouble keeping my *nostrils* above water, let alone my entire head.

Today, a lifetime later, I am much better at purposely screening out conversations that take place at the table next to me in a restaurant. But I struggled throughout my college years with this screening malady and was fairly unsuccessful in changing it.

The other big roadblock was the size of the university, about 10,000 students strong, and what a campus that size lacks. For me, the place was terrifyingly impersonal. I couldn't seem to find my niche, a place I could grab on to and hold and make my own for the duration.

Moving among those hundreds, even thousands, of students as they milled around on campus; living in a dorm surrounded by other students on every side; attending classes that were filled with students, sometimes in lecture halls of several hundred; even having a roommate—I still felt alone. I felt like I was on my own, searching for an anchor in a turbulent sea. I knew one or two students in most of my classes, I certainly knew students in my dorm, and I had classmates I could have the standard cup of bad coffee with. I could walk into the student union, the campus coffeeshop/cafeteria/meeting place/hangout, at just about any time of the day or night and see members of various student cliques huddled together over coffee and nasty dishes of cigarette butts or some kind of gray food, laughing, relaxing, or engaged in serious conversation. I took a small measure of pride in the fact that I could sit with groups of nearly any ilk—the Young Socialists, the Student Democrats, the civil rights activists, the antiwar advocates—and someone would recognize me; I could join the group without feeling like an intruder. The discussions could be stimulating, challenging, heady—often I would leave with an adrenaline high. But that sense of comradeship always tended to be ephemeral, not lasting to the next time I encountered one of the individuals. Not that I would have to reintroduce myself with each new encounter, but the previous moment of closeness, that moment of shared recognition, was gone and would have to be re-created. To me, it felt as though we might as well be meeting for the first time again and again; none of it seemed genuine or sincere or made to last.

We were all living, it seemed to me, in a temporary world that would end in four years, at which point we would go our separate ways—to fabulous jobs, to a marriage, or to some other exciting adventure. And then what? Would we ever see each other again? Share a laugh together again? Wonder about dating or friends or the fate of the world with each other ever again? In this impersonal and temporary setting, I doubted it. It seemed like everyone was playing it safe and avoiding getting too close in the first place. Maybe that was just my projection. Or maybe we, all of us in our callow youth, were still figuring out *how* to get close.

Thank goodness there were exceptions, even for me. It was at CU that I made one lifelong friend. She always seemed happy to see me, always had time to talk to me; we could engage in stimulating conversations not only about our classes but also about ourselves, our lives, and the greater world around us. We had fun together, and she made me laugh. We remain close even today, though we live in different cities and in the past have lived in different states. And she still makes me laugh. She was the antithesis of the impersonal that was thwarting me, and that was enough to help me make it to graduation. Our friendship has kept me from believing that the much-touted lifelong college friendship was strictly another college myth.

Aside from making one true friend, that was my close-to-miserable college experience. Today, I understand it differently. After a lifetime of engagement with issues of personal identity, race and gender biases, and oppression, I can say that my misery was more than self-indulgent, college-age angst. It was my internal, mostly invisible struggle with a divided self. The division for me appeared to be just the opposite of what the majority of Asian and especially Japanese American students scurrying around on campus were experiencing. Most of them had grown up in some form of Asian American community, so they needed to figure out how to interface with a mostly white world. They were stuck on campus, too, and couldn't retreat back to the comfort of their neighborhoods, familiar friends, and favorite haunts. My experience growing up in white America allowed me to act as though I fit in socially with white students. But internally I was constantly mediating between the polite social rules I had learned at home and the very different but completely acceptable social rules of the mainstream. I was described by the white mainstream as polite, quiet, a good listener, thoughtful, a nice person, barely noticed in a crowd except that I stood out physically as the only "minority" there. Not a person of particular interest, certainly not a person to be reckoned with in any way.

In conversations with a group of white students, I did my best to inter-ject comments, to be an active participant; I laughed at the jokes and looked enthusiastic about deciding on a place to go for coffee outside the student union. I went along with the small talk about drunken parties or outrageous behavior. And by the end of the four years, I was tired of being so agreeable and invisible.

When I was with a group of Asian students, I got tired of wondering if I was being too loud or too assertive, if I spoke up too quickly, or if I looked like I wasn't enthusiastic enough about being part of the group.

I never seemed to get a break from switching back and forth between the two worlds. I was tired of trying to fit in everywhere and feeling like I fit in nowhere. I was glad to be graduating, which I did manage to pull off—with a less than stellar academic record, another departure from the stereotype of the Asian American student.

Nearly a decade later, I got a job that put me back on the campus of my alma mater and would eventually point me toward graduate school and a career. I had been recruited for the position of assistant director for an edu-cational opportunity program (EOP) for Asian American students. The pro-gram was established to provide ancillary services to help them get through college and graduate, degree in hand. There were parallel programs for the African American, Native American, and Latino students on campus.

The creation of such a program for the so-called model minority student group would seem to raise questions: If Asian American students were truly the model minority, why would they need such a program? What could an EOP possibly provide them? Wouldn't it be a waste of time and money? The need for additional services for the other student minority groups, the argu-ment went, made good historical sense; the time was long overdue, in fact, to give those students all the help they needed to be successful in obtaining a college degree. This was, after all, the early 1970s, and the civil rights struggle was still raging in the country. The existence of equal opportunity programs at CU and elsewhere was proof that the Civil Rights Movement's struggle for equality had even penetrated the ivory towers of academia.

In this climate, Asian American students fought back against their assigned stereotype and demanded an EOP to suit their needs. They saw themselves as kin to their fellow people of color, and they wanted their share of the pie. Further, they did not see getting their slice of the pie as a competition with the other programs. No one would have to be edged out. In the end, the directors of the various CU programs worked collaboratively with each other, and respectful bonds were forged. They truly understood the power of standing together. Our students likewise took pride in standing with their compatriots in a coalition of color. This collective unity might have been a first for most of the students in all of the programs.

For more than one reason, I was an unusual choice for assistant director of the Asian American EOP. It was not just because I happened to have majored in English: it seemed like none of my personal history fit the typical Asian American or even Japanese American profile. Starting as far back as my birth in rural Wyoming, I seemed to lack the common thread that wove Japanese Americans together into a single cloth. That missing thread, of course, was the fact that although my parents had been evacuated along with everyone else, they had never been in a Japanese American concentration camp during World War II.

Not having to go to a camp turned out to be a double-edged sword: my parents had escaped incarceration, but they had also lost the benefit of having any community support from their natural peer group. It was the beginning of a path that would forever set them apart from their peers, a path that rarely seemed to intersect with another Asian face. At the end of the war and upon release from the camps, the majority of the Japanese returned to the West Coast to rebuild their communities, restart former businesses, return to school and college, and start their lives over in the places they were familiar with and felt connected to, even after such a wrenching removal.

But my father had been farming throughout the war, and he was trying to make a go of it. He was in no position to suddenly, because of an arbitrary date, walk away from all he had been building and return—with his now much larger family—to Seattle, where he had nothing. He had made his commitment: he was now a farmer.

This very detached personal background of mine, so different from—indeed, almost at odds with—the standard Asian American experience, could have been the very reason I was chosen for a job with the Asian American EOP. It was a time when politics had invaded every corner of the university, and that was true for all the EOPs as well. I may have gotten the job precisely because I had no political history with the "community," no political enemies; folks were looking for neutral ground, for someone without the baggage acquired from being a standout political activist in that community during those tumultuous times. Someone who could come into the arena with a fresh perspective and no political debts to repay.

Of course, I had been paying attention and I knew the issues people were hotly debating. I knew why Asian American students shied away from English, history, and other humanities classes; I knew what the EOP could give them that they would be hard-pressed to find elsewhere; and I knew why they needed what the program could give them.

In short, I knew the Asian American EOP would give our students a group to be a part of. It wasn't by chance that Asians settled in this country in groups, making the journey together. Once here, they found other groups with the help of friends and relatives who had arrived before them. They formed knots of their own communities in cities all across the country but especially where they had landed: along the West Coast. They banded together in large urban areas, the Chinatowns, J-Towns, Little Tokyos, and, later, Koreatowns found in San Francisco and Los Angeles and Seattle. They formed farming communities in the central valley of California and in western states like Montana, Idaho, Oregon, Washington, Wyoming, and the Dakotas. They stuck together and helped each other survive.

The supreme irony of the concentration camps built to punish and isolate Japanese Americans during World War II was that they allowed the incarcerees to remain together, to continue their lives in some form of group-ness, even though some friends and neighbors had been separated from each other and put into different camps. These were people who could adapt to this new form of group living because they valued the contact and understood the importance of remaining a group. This is not to paint a picture of complete harmony among the residents. They were, after all, human beings with human feelings and conflicts. But taken as a complete phenomenon and as a situation in which those incarcerated had absolutely no choice or voice, the Japanese American incarceration camps became communities that made the most and best of an illegal and dehumanizing predicament. On the whole, there was little internal conflict that wasn't resolved quietly among the residents of the camp in question. And the baseball leagues, dance bands, art, and cultural activities formed in the various camps have become their own phenomena and the topics of books, television specials, and public talks over the years since the end of the war. After the war, the majority of Japanese

Americans returned to the West Coast and rebuilt their urban communities or returned to farming in states they were familiar with—and as before, before the camps and, earlier, in the old country, they stuck together and they survived.

For Asian American students, the EOP center offered them similar comforts, filled familiar needs. It gave them a place to gather and relax, to snatch a break from the need and pressure to always speak up, show they existed, show they were important persons in their own right and could stand out. It gave them a break from the Copernicus axiom, which for most Asian kids had not been the governing principle with which they were raised. Fundamentally, it was a program that would let them retain their sense of group-ness. But operating underneath, it was also a safe place for them to practice expressing their differences, to learn to have a civil disagreement with someone and feel safe about it, to learn to challenge each other's thinking and ideas—skills their white peers seemed to have been born with. We never named it this way, but the sub-rosa skill they were learning was how one thought, talked, and acted like an "individual." Our Western cultural archetype is the hero, the one who acts alone or with minimal help in slaying the dragon, blinding the Cyclops, or seeking out and conquering the enemy, whatever its form. We have idolized the rugged individual, going at least as far back as the ancient Greeks, and this idolization experienced a particularly lively revival in the Wild West of America. But in Japan, the kamikaze pilot took his nosedive to destruction not to gain personal glory or a personal place in history but for the good and glory of the nation. The samurai was a mighty warrior who honed his individual skills, but he was first and foremost a member of a clan, and his loyalty lay with his clan and its master. In Chinese, Japanese, and Korean scroll paintings, the human beings are tiny figures at the bottom, taking a considerable back seat to the mountains, rivers, and forests that cover most of the scroll. They have their place in a much bigger picture.

Our students liked being at the Asian American EOP office, and the rooms of the little cottage that housed us were always filled with at least a few students; during hours when few classes were in session, they were often crowded. The cottage itself enhanced the feeling that once inside, each person was home and could let her or his hair down, relax, let go of the pressure to talk a lot or defend or explain, stop trying to be unique. One could blend in, and that would be just fine.

Of course, those students also got help with their academics. One very popular service matched them with tutors, and I noticed that tutors for English classes were in particularly high demand. Sociology classes were growing in popularity among our students, but it was clear that they were still not majoring in English or in classes that required a lot of writing or verbal skills. As an English major much their senior in age, who had graduated a decade before from this same university, I found this lopsided trend all too familiar. I recognized it from my time as a student here. Had so little changed? But my time with the program soon convinced me that this opposition between the group and the individual is what creates the largest gap between the cultures of Asia and the cultures of Europe and North America. Because this important difference is not concrete, because it is not physical like eye shape or height or one's name, it can be confounding to everyone—even the individuals experiencing it. Our students may not have been able to verbally name this difference, but it might well have been the main reason they liked coming to the cottage and being in the program. They felt safe, seen, and understood without saying much. They felt no pressure to talk their way into recognition; they didn't feel the need to engage in stimulating intellectual conversation; they seemed to enjoy being around each other, having a few laughs, and getting academic help when needed. Somehow the idea of needing to talk, talk, talk about everything all the time was not part of their personal, cultural, or academic DNA.

I was enthusiastic about working with Asian American students because I knew intimately what a bad college experience could feel like. I wanted to help make their experience a much better one than my own. Maybe, with the proper support, these students could organize their time, find the right majors, and, most important, cast aside negative stereotypes and see themselves through a new and positive cultural lens. Maybe I secretly felt as though I would get a chance to do college over again and this time enjoy it.

Of course, I didn't and couldn't do my college experience over again, but I was pleasantly surprised to find that, like our students, I also did well in our program's environment. At first I felt a little wary about being back on campus, but the feeling didn't last because I was excited by what I was tasked to do. Part of my job was to help establish special classes for our students, especially basic writing skills. I was thrilled to be able to help students in this area in which I had some background and where I knew they often floundered.

I was also tasked to help them think ahead to what might be out there for them after graduation, how best to use that new degree. What kind of job? Maybe graduate school?

I needed to interact not only with students but also with levels of administrators in the various academic departments. And it was a big bonus for me to be in a position to interact with the other EOP administrators and some of their students as well. I was learning to feel comfortable and to have fun with the African Americans, Latinos, and Native Americans on campus. I hardly ever had interactions with white students, the kids I had felt surrounded by when I was a student at CU.

I was seduced. Where before I had felt overwhelmed, pulled in two directions by my separate worlds and at odds with all the activity and stimulation, I now was energized and I wanted more. It was this job—my close involvement with students and my different and adult involvement with academia—that made me want to find permanent work on a university campus. But I was fast learning that university professors are another group who prefers being surrounded by its own. In other words, to be taken seriously on a university campus, one needed a higher degree, something more than a bachelor's, which was the bare minimum. I was getting the message: I needed to go to graduate school.

Until I had come upon a practical reason for going to graduate school, I had never seriously considered it. It had seemed like something that was too expensive, took too many years, and required committing to a world that seemed ultimately to relate only to itself. It was easy to find graduate students on campus to talk to because so many of them had been on campus for years—finishing research; traveling to research sites, sometimes in offbeat destinations; writing their dissertations; trying to satisfy a fussy or temperamental professor on their research/dissertation committee. It seemed like a lot to subject oneself to. But suddenly, here I was, wanting to be a part of that crowd engaged in the life of academia. The questions became: What subject should I study, and what kind of degree was I looking for? I still wanted to do something practical, something that kept me in what I considered the real world. I didn't think I wanted to commit to the time demands of a PhD. That required far too many years, and financially I needed to get back to work as soon as I could. Another six or more years as a student on campus was out of the question. Besides, even if I liked the research aspect of the work, teaching, as I learned early on, was not a good fit for me: I could literally put people to sleep in the classroom. I should probably go for a two-year program, a master's degree in something practical.

When the pupil is ready, the teacher will appear. I don't remember when or where I first heard that pithy old proverb. But in the case of graduate school, the proverb proved true. Having landed in the white world in junior high and never looked back, I had learned one unequivocal lesson: that I needed to talk, to talk about *everything*. Especially anything I could use some help with. So I began to tell people around me that I was going to leave the Asian American EOP program and go to graduate school. Naturally, since I was working on a college campus, those people had ideas and opinions on what to study and where to do it. I was leaning toward social work because it fit my requirements: it involved a two-year program, provided a way to keep working intimately with people, and offered flexibility, with different job options available in the field. Maybe I could even find a job similar to the one I would be leaving. The one troublesome hurdle I had to overcome was the popular, stereotyped image of the "social worker," the matronly female with spectacles, a stern look, and granny shoes. (I loved shopping for shoes, but granny shoes were definitely not in my picture.) She would go to a welfare mother's apartment, march up the front steps, and, after entering the home, go first to the bedroom and check under the bed. If no man was hiding there, she could assume that the mother was not getting financial help from a man on the sly, so she could then turn over the (too meager) welfare check for the family. This was the prevailing myth of what social workers did. This is not what I wanted to do or how I wanted to be thought of.

What helped me make up my mind and finally choose social work was a conversation I had with a woman in the profession. It was an unplanned, spontaneous conversation, and I don't remember why we were talking, since she was not someone I was close to or who had dealings with our program. She must have been the teacher who appeared, the one predicted by the proverb. Carol was African American, cultured, cosmopolitan, and well-spoken. She told me I should specialize in clinical (also called psychiatric) social work. That way my main task would be to provide psychotherapy for individuals. I could go into private practice if I wanted to, meaning I could have my own office and see clients on an individual basis as an MD in private practice would. I was sold! No checking under beds for the errant male. No denying welfare checks to the mother who was barely holding it together. If I wanted, I could open my own office anywhere, or if I wanted to work for an organization, that would also be possible. Carol gave me the name of a small school back East that had a good clinical social work program.

Now, with a clear direction, I set to work contacting schools and filling out applications. Filling out a form, a form of any import, has always felt like a major trial to me. Coming face to face with one, I feel immediately overwhelmed and have to fight against the inertia that overtakes me. I can't remember when this feeling started, but I can't remember ever feeling differently about filling out a form. Now, suddenly, I was faced with piles of forms—some with bubbles to darken, others with lots of blank lines to fill in, still others with two or three questions, each followed by enough blank space to write a convincing, concise little paragraph.

I had really hoped that graduate school would be my ticket back to California; I had never given up the dream of returning to the Bay area. But when I got the application for the social work school at UC Berkeley, I just couldn't handle what seemed to me like endless sheets of paper. I kept shuffling the papers around but could never fill them out. When I got the application for the school Carol had mentioned to me, I was shocked and thrilled: an application consisting of a single page! I filled it out, wrote the obligatory statement of intent, and sent it off with a sigh of relief. Much to my even greater surprise and relief, a few months later I received a letter of acceptance from the school, Simmons College, to its School of Social Work. People think I am joking when I tell them I chose my graduate school based on its one-page application form.

Simmons College is a small, private formerly women's college in Boston that had only begun accepting men around the time I applied. This was during the mid-1970s, just before all the money for grants and scholarships had dried up and the only way to go on to school was to go into debt. For a change, my timing was spot-on, and I landed a grant that enabled me to go to a private institution. I had never been to Boston or to New England, but I had seen pictures of New England towns in *Life* magazine in our Montana farmhouse, and I had held on to my desire to experience firsthand the region's glorious autumn colors. That part didn't disappoint: the fall colors my first year were spectacular. Who knew that leaves could turn so many shades of red and yellow—from light, bright reds all the way through the spectrum to deep magentas and from weak yellows spreading into nearly blinding golds. The air was crisp and tingly. It was perfect autumn weather. (I had yet to experience a New England winter.)

Boston has one of the largest Chinatowns in the United States. But my school was, once again, mostly white. There was a sprinkling of Black faces, but in my class, my two-year cohort, I remember only two Asian faces—my own and that of K, a Japanese woman from Japan. She had been in the United States for several years and her English was quite good, even if she had an accent. The professors and other students would regularly confuse me for her, although rarely the other way around because, I suspect, she fulfilled their expectations more completely: her accent gave her away immediately as not American-born. I might have looked foreign, but mostly, if K and I were compared, I would come out as more like my white classmates. K and I were in many of the same classes, so I got to know her somewhat, but she also seemed foreign to me, mostly because I thought she was clearly trying to act "American"—which I saw in her assertiveness, her eagerness to speak out, her behavior bordering almost on pushy or brash. Not at all the shy, retiring Asian female stereotype. If anything, I fit that mold better. Even if K had not been Japanese, I would have read her the same way. She was not someone I could feel close to.

Psychotherapy is dubbed "the talking cure." Two people sit in a room a comfortable distance apart, facing each other. The door is closed tight, and the room may have extra soundproofing. They talk privately for fifty minutes, or, more precisely, one of them does a lot of the talking while the other listens patiently and empathically and asks questions or interjects salient comments at key moments in the conversation.

This is a pretty accurate picture of what a therapy session looks like. However, the very idea of going to talk to a complete stranger to tell her or him about your most personal problems, to talk about your parents and your family relationships, to mention sex, and then to tell how you *feel* about all these deeply personal things—if that is a leap of trust for many white people, it is even more so for people of color. After all, for much of the "minority" population in the United States, the white world represents "the man," and that kind of talk is not what one does with "the man." Yet as therapists, that's exactly what we were learning to do: to dig into, muck around in these very intimate corners of another individual's life. Encourage the person in the other chair to talk about all of it.

For African Americans, from the earliest beginnings of our country and especially as a result of slavery, one unwritten rule for survival was *not* to reveal anything personal or truly of oneself to anyone in the white mainstream. I believe Asian American culture has similar rules, partly due to culture and partly because of our collective history in America. It seemed to me that those deeply personal conversations—revealing interior angst, conflicts with and between parents, financial issues facing the family, anything having to do with sex—none of these were topics to be shared outside the home and certainly not with a stranger. Yet it was this attitude that justified to the white world their way of seeing people of color as shy or withholding or nonverbal or sullen—or maybe just not very bright—when they were seen outside their own groups. Yet when in their groups, people of color were criticized for being loud or rowdy. Suddenly, they felt threatening to white people, who were accustomed to seeing the subdued side when *they* were in control. It seemed like there was a huge trench between the world of the white mainstream, the Anglo world—the world of psychology and psychotherapists—and the world whose cultures didn't make talking, telling all, their top social priority.

So where did that leave me? Where did I fit into this seeming divide? It looked like once again I was caught, trapped between two worlds with opposing social behaviors. For many people of color, the two worlds exist, but in their souls they belong to the world of their own kind—usually the world they grew up in—and they find ways to navigate their way through the other, white world. For me, having lost my Japanese community as a youngster and being left with no alternative but to live surrounded by white people, I felt I belonged to both worlds equally, that I fit into and understood them both. I knew that people who didn't know me would see me and categorize me, put me in my Asian box. But they would soon find out that that was not the only place I belonged. Sometimes I could see the surprise on their faces when they found me as literate in and about the white world as they were. The painful and discouraging part for me was that internally, these worlds still clashed; in some instances there remained that 180 degree polarization and I, because I saw both sides, was left to decide which way to jump.

Prior to my training in psychotherapy, I had seen myself as someone who enjoyed talking, having good conversations with people I knew—although I still found it hard to jump into a lively conversation in groups of three or more white people. I always marveled that in groups like this, each person seemed to know exactly when to chime in and add their comment and that before there was a pause, someone else had already begun to speak in response. The conversation seemed to flow along like a fast-moving stream—and rather than jumping in, I was still trying to find that accessible spot where I could slowly wade in. Or at least that's how it felt to me. I found these situations frustrating, but overall, I didn't feel incompetent socially when it came to having a conversation. In fact, I relied on my verbal ability as the primary way of fitting myself into the white mainstream. When it came to thinking about graduate school, I wasn't particularly nervous about starting a new adventure in a new city. I'd done that before and had managed to fit in well enough to get along and to get what I could out of the new experience. But learning to do therapy was akin to going from the farm team to a professional ball club.

Thankfully, I was ready and eager to learn. I was open to the school, to the city, to the new breed of student I was meeting—mostly extremely verbal East Coast urbanites and suburbanites—and to taking on a new profession and a new identity. My classes were not that big, usually fewer than twenty students, which enhanced the possibility that everyone would get a chance to speak a lot, in class. Which my classmates did without hesitation. My own default mode when I have to learn something new is to watch and listen. Which is what I mostly did, at least at first.

I don't think I really understood how therapy worked before I got to grad school. Shortly after starting my program, when I learned that I would be expected to begin providing therapy for people almost immediately, I didn't believe it. I had no idea our clinical training, our internships, began in our first year of school and continued until we graduated. I now know that this strategy makes for a good program because each new intern receives the maximum amount of training with real "patients" (the word used at school and at most of the placements) and receives close supervision of his or her work with each patient throughout the entire two years. But at the time, I was thrown completely off guard. Not wanting to look ignorant or naive, I didn't tell anyone how I was feeling: I felt scared and at a loss. How does one even begin to be the therapist, to be the one in the other chair? I think the school may have had an assumption that was never voiced: surely, anyone who wanted to be a therapist had experienced therapy, had had a positive experience and received help and wanted to provide that help to someone else. Surely, anyone who wanted to be a therapist knew firsthand what went on behind that closed door and was ready to recapitulate the scene.

Unfortunately, I was not that person. I had never engaged in long-term psychotherapy. In the few weeks of classes before we went to our internships, I tried desperately to imagine, to visualize, to hear a therapy session in my mind. I can't deny that I had a shaky beginning, but at least I knew from the start that when I was feeling the most unsure, my best bet was to keep quiet and listen.

My classes at Simmons were a magnification of every class I had ever attended where speaking up, voicing one's opinion and understanding of the situation, and sounding intelligent mattered. This was especially true in the classes that had to do with case discussions. While there are some who believe that the study of human behavior has no clear scientific basis and is just a bunch of description and speculation, we were given psychological theory starting with Freud and going forward. We discussed human behavior from various theoretical perspectives. We learned how to determine truly pathological behavior from clinical neurosis and from the minor neurotic things we all do from time to time in everyday life. We learned about Freud and what he contributed to the field besides those distorted jokes about penis envy. It took a while not to feel intimidated every time we entered the class taught by his honest-to-goodness granddaughter, although she never made a big deal about her psychological lineage. (Once when a brave student asked her what it was like growing up with her grandfather, she joked that sometimes she thought she would have preferred growing up with Erik Erikson.) And like medical students, I am told, most of us re-diagnosed ourselves with each new psychological problem we encountered.

What continued to be consistent is that the way we learned was to discuss thoroughly every aspect of every case in every class. I had probably never talked as much or listened as carefully as I did in those case discussions at Simmons. There is a particular language that goes with these discussions, specific words like "clearly" and "supportive" and "separation" and "individuation," to name a few of the most frequently used. Even though I had gone to all-white schools in the past, almost from the first classroom I had entered; even though I had hung around with groups of white friends; even though I had participated in white student groups and other kinds of social groups as an adult, nothing had prepared me for training in the "talking cure."

Every little detail of a patient's life was parsed, dissected, thoroughly examined in microscopic detail, all through the vehicle of language. Of words. Starting with how one entered the room, sat in the chair, did or did not give eye contact, how easy or difficult it was for the person to express herself or himself, the person's class and educational level, and the specific details of that individual's story. Even if the patient were eighty years old, questions about their parents and family of origin were typically asked.

At first I thought this degree of probing was intrusive and unnecessary: Your mother's worst reprimand when she got mad at you? Your grandparents came from what little village in Portugal? Your older brother had how many friends in junior high? But the more I understood the process of psychotherapy, the better I understood the necessity of asking lots of questions like these. A physicist or chemist viewing the world would be asking an entirely different set of questions. But a therapist needs as much personal information and detail as possible to help the person sitting before him or her solve their problems. This is how the pieces of the puzzle of their life begin to coalesce.

Nevertheless, there were plenty of times in my classes when I thought my classmates were dissecting the individual so finely that they were talking just for the pleasure of hearing themselves sound brilliant in front of their classmates. There also were times when I thought the entire profession and what it did was useful only if one were well educated and upper-middle to upper class and could talk about anything with complete ease and comfort—and most important, if the person, the patient, believed in the power of words. In my experience, this was typically the description of a white person. More often than I wanted to, I was the student who had to point out that not all cultures might see things the same way. For example, would neurotic behavior always look the same, no matter the client's cultural background? I knew there were differences, though I didn't have the answers as to what to look for in every different culture of color. I didn't even know what those major differences might be in Japanese culture and how they might have morphed when the Japanese became more westernized by living in the United States. What aspects of the original culture were still operating and influencing the individual, and what had been completely erased? And what about other cultures of color and other non-Anglo, newly immigrant white cultures? How did the received psychological framework stand up then?

It was up to me to point out specific examples of my concerns: for example, that Asian people did not necessarily give automatic eye contact because it was impolite to do so, especially if the other person was older or had more social standing; that in a conversation involving several people, Asian people did not feel it was polite to look for the first crack in the conversation and leap in with their comments; that Japanese people did not usually accept refreshments at someone's home the first time they were offered, which didn't mean they didn't want any, only that the ritual required coaxing on the part of the hostess. Were any similar behaviors seen in other, non-Asian cultures? The Boston area had communities of Portuguese and Greeks and Italians. What did they think about going to therapy? Did any similar behaviors characterize these populations?

I was opening the door to some questions that didn't come up very often and that could affect more than the way Asian cultures responded to therapy. I was not loud or brash or confrontational when I posed my questions and concerns; I was truly trying to find out how I was to understand what I was expected to learn and do and how I was to try to do it with efficacy. And I didn't always pose my questions to professors. Sometimes they were just ones I struggled with internally or maybe asked of a clinical supervisor at my internship or talked about with a fellow student. These were not questions that were automatically part of the curricula in any of my classes. There were also no hard, fast answers, but at least the discussion had been sparked.

For the most part, I went along with the curricula. The challenge and therefore the learning took place in working with real patients. I learned I could listen to others with empathy as well as understanding and thus help them along their path. I learned to look at myself and what my own issues were as I went about my business in the world, how not to get my "stuff" confused with the "stuff" of the patient—perhaps the single most useful part of training as a therapist. With time and practice, I got over feeling like it was impolite and intrusive to be asking so many personal questions. I knew language was the primary tool, and I was glad I didn't feel awkward about having a serious discussion about something. It didn't take too long for me to feel like I had made a good career choice.

Simmons gave no letter grades, only professor evaluations of each student at the end of each class. At the end of two years, none of my evaluations questioned my ability to graduate and enter the world as a therapist. I would graduate in good standing.

Right after graduation, I was lucky to be hired by a community mental health center in Denver. In those days, the mid-1970s, community mental health centers, established under President John F. Kennedy, existed in many larger cities. These centers were established to serve the average, everyday person who might be suffering from a common mental disorder like depression, suicidal thoughts, trouble in a marriage, trouble with a child, psychosis. The help would be professional, would cover a range of services, and would be affordable. The concept behind these centers was that everyone, not just the wealthy, should have access to decent mental health services. It was a radical idea at the time, since the stereotypes of the mentally ill and their service providers were anything but accurate or complimentary. The mentally ill person was usually portrayed as a scary, shifty-eyed criminal type; a disheveled, filthy street person; or someone so out of control that they were dangerous to encounter. In these imaginings, they were usually locked in a small cell or chained to a bed in a big room along with others of the same ilk. In more upscale settings, the doctor or provider might be a man sitting behind a huge desk looking anything but interested in his patient who was sitting in a chair on the other side of the desk; or maybe the provider was sitting off to the side of a couch, pad and pencil on his lap, looking bored and barely awake as the patient—often a woman—lay on the couch, staring wide-eyed into space as she rambled on endlessly.

Community mental health centers changed those damning images by bringing an accurate face to mental illness and its treatment. This was a good place for me to begin my career, since I was still not convinced internally that psychotherapy was a service that most people, especially poorer ones or people of color, could relate to. This first job would give me a chance to test the belief that it was. The other piece of luck was that I would get to work with the other Asian American therapists at the center who had come together and formed a team. The team's mission was to find ways to make psychological services relevant and useful to the Asian and Asian American populations.

We were a small team—just five clinicians, though that was more in one place than I had ever encountered—and there were few established markers as to how to do things: we were helping to create them, and that was exciting to me. One of our luckiest breaks was that one of our team members was a

Japanese MD, a psychiatrist. He spoke excellent English, and one of his consuming interests was cross-cultural psychology. His credentials were impeccable, including not only Harvard but the Harvard, Princeton, and Yale of Japan combined: Tokyo University. But what I liked most about Matt (Dr. N to his colleagues) were his gentle humanitarianism and his sense of humor. Under his guidance and status as a psychiatrist, we created an outreach clinic for newly arrived Vietnamese, Hmong, and Laotian refugees, mostly peasant farmers who had been relocated to Denver. Their collective community was large and growing. They were part of the "collateral damage," the horrifying aftermath of the fall of Saigon in the spring of 1975. They were fleeing their countries and now, barely a year later, had ended up in Denver.

Our first outreach clinic was held on a cold winter evening someplace in the refugees' general neighborhood in Denver. I remember that the room was filled with people, only a few of whom had any knowledge of or facility in English. I looked around at the slightly motley-looking group, who were staring at our group of "helpers," and saw the wrinkled, weather-beaten faces of the elders, the concerned and slightly more hopeful faces of the men and women who could have been their middle-aged adult children, and only a sprinkling of youths or adolescents. At the first sight of this group of displaced, confused, melancholy people, my heart skipped a beat. How could we possibly help them? What could we do to improve their tragically interrupted, broken lives? How could we even talk with them? A few of the refugees had been in the area longer than most of the people we met that night. These old-timers, for want of a better word, were able to help with translating our English into their native tongues. But the language of psychology can be complex and can sound and feel stilted, even to a native English speaker. Looking at the group, looking hard at their faces, looking into their eyes—some were leaking a few discreet tears—it wasn't difficult for any of us on the team to make an initial diagnosis: the depression in the room was nearly stifling. It sat like an evil spirit encompassing its victims, tamping them down, almost paralyzing them. Dr. N began slowly, and with the help of an interpreter he was able to painstakingly unravel the story of one of the most depressed-looking elders—his story of leaving his country under fear of being killed, being rescued by American soldiers, sent by plane to the United States, and then landing here in Denver with nothing, not even all his family. He was glad to be alive, and he was grateful to the Americans.

But there was so much missing: not just his family and friends but his country, his way of life, his livelihood.

I listened and filled in the blanks: What could he do now that he had no land, no money, no job, couldn't speak the language, had never learned to read in his own language and so would not be likely to learn to read English? Now he was an old man stranded in a city that could turn freezing cold for long stretches of time. He would never again see the palm trees or the verdant green of the land, pick the fruit hanging from the branches of trees, feel the heat of the day envelop him year-round, see the rain come down in sheets around him. Cruelly separated from friends and family, he was destined to die alone in some strange, cold, and snowy foreign land with no one to properly bury him and mourn him. I was heartbroken. I wasn't too successful at keeping an emotional clinical distance from these dejected souls. The slow unraveling of story after story revealed much the same information.

Dr. N did what he could by methodically, meticulously, thoroughly obtaining enough personal history to very, very carefully prescribe appropriate doses of antidepressant medication. Through the translator he explained how to take the pills. He told them he would be back in a few days to check on them, to see how they were faring.

As the door closed behind us and our team members walked together out into the frigid night air, I knew I wasn't the only one wondering about the possibility of suicides. Wondering how many of those mournful souls were broken enough to attempt to end their suffering by taking their own lives. We didn't know and couldn't do the usual thorough assessments. We would have to be extra watchful.

For many months, Dr. N and members of our team followed up on the refugee group. I would be thrilled if I could report that our clinic cured them all of their overwhelming sadness and depression. That, however, would be a gross exaggeration of reality. The medication and their contact with us as caring helpers did play a part in helping some feel better, but the needs of people experiencing the level of loss felt by any refugee group are extreme. Simultaneous with our work, a host of other community resources were mobilized to help with housing, English-language learning, medical aid, community meetings to help the refugees come together and find ways to empower themselves and each other. Their new country, town, and community were trying to help them put back together the pieces of their lives shattered from the cost of war off the battlefield—the cost usually hidden from view. The cost of collateral damage.

I spent two years at the community mental health center working with the team, trying to improve services to the Asian and Asian American populations.

In community mental health, one truly sees the full spectrum of mental health disorders, so I was also becoming more seasoned as a psychotherapist in general. I learned to work in crisis mode with people who needed to be seen that same day or something terrible could befall them, or they might do something terrible to themselves; I learned to understand more about that all-pervasive problem of depression and how to work with the varying degrees of it; I learned to work with people who thought about killing themselves, who were close to killing themselves, who had already tried to kill themselves and were now, or maybe once again, seeking help; and I learned to work with disgruntled people in unhappy relationships, jobs, families. I often felt the weight of the work, but I was learning and doing and becoming more skilled in how to talk with my patients: what questions to ask and how to ask them, how to listen to their answers and let those responses guide me in what more to ask and how. I was watching as well as experiencing in real time the benefit, actually the necessity, of seeking out the tiny details of a situation or story, of not offhandedly disregarding some piece of information as unimportant. Along with the powerful tool of listening, the therapist watches closely the person across from her, feels empathy with the person, but still relies most heavily on the tool of language, of words, to engage with the person in the process of healing. I was finally convinced that the talking cure really worked by talking, and I was happy to be doing what I was doing.

I had never completely given up on returning to the San Francisco Bay area. The area was physically beautiful with the hills, the bay, and that charming, exotic city, "Baghdad by the Bay." The weather was mild and temperate. But for me the real pull was the fact that the Bay area had a history of Asian Americans and that they continued to live there in significant numbers and relative ease. After incarceration, the Japanese American population had returned to the cities of the Bay area, reconstituted their lives, and once again created thriving communities. It was not only the numbers of people who looked like me but the fact that looking like me was one version of looking normal. It wasn't a big deal to have Asian markets, Asian restaurants, Asian American teachers, doctors, dentists, store clerks, artists, librarians, and so forth. They could be seen everywhere. Better yet, they could be left alone; they were not hassled or picked on or belittled or threatened. For someone still struggling with where I belonged in Asian America, given the anomaly that was my family's history, I imagined such an environment would feel like a way to fit in for now while I figured out how I was to truly fit in. I could catch a break from making a big deal out of my ethnicity; I could relax and just be myself without drawing attention to myself.

So when a friend told me about a job opening in San Francisco, I lost no time sending in my application. Maybe it was fate or just plain good luck, but I got the job and soon found myself back in the Bay area. Once again, I was nowhere near a college campus, my long-term goal. To the contrary, I was working with parents and families at a preschool modeled after Head Start. I didn't mind. I liked the idea of working once again with young children—with kids getting ready for grade school—a throwback to my days as a VISTA volunteer. I believed in the theory that kids who got a good start in school did better overall and dropped out less often. The school was located in the South of Market District, which at that time was nothing like the spiffed-up, gentrified area it is today. The majority of the children were of color—African American and Latino/Hispanic—and some were from the white working class. I felt comfortable there, talking with parents, getting to know them and their children, and feeling like I also was accepted by them.

Being at the preschool program in San Francisco was the beginning of my actual adult life in the area. I loved being there, and the Bay area definitely had a grip on me. I finally had to acknowledge in my itinerant soul that this was truly my home.

I continued doing psychotherapy and eventually made it back to a college campus, the University of California at Berkeley, where I worked with students who were bright, lively, and sometimes tragic, their stories spanning the broad spectrum of mental health problems: trauma; physical, sexual, and emotional abuse; depression; suicidal thoughts and feelings; a total disconnect from the real world; addiction; identity questions; roommate and other relationship troubles; dysfunctional family systems; professors they couldn't get along with; questions about the meaning of life. Despite the too-often heartrending stories they revealed about their lives and what brought them into therapy, the students were young, filled with hope, courageous, and motivated—and they believed that getting help now would prevent disaster

later in their lives. They tackled their therapy sessions with the same determination and commitment with which they tackled everything in their lives
at that energetic young age. Working with them gave me, however ironic
this may sound, hope for the future. I grew to love the students and my work
and having to go back onto a college campus every day.

Yet I admit, this highly suspect talking cure still faces a slow and winding
road toward being understood and fully accepted in Asian American communities. Sitting with a stranger to whom you tell your most personal hopes
and secrets still seems like an alien, if not unacceptable, activity to many
Asian people. Can they fully trust that idea of "confidentiality"—and what
does it mean in the first place? How can anyone who has never met you until
now even begin to understand or help you? Worst of all, to call this field of
study a science seems like stretching something already questionable into
pure mythology. Or fabrication. Or self-delusion.

Back in the mid-1990s, my clinic at Berkeley invited Dr. Stanley Sue to
speak to our staff. In the field of psychology and especially in cross-cultural
psychology, Dr. Sue, a Chinese American, had built quite a reputation and
name for himself. Nearly twenty years earlier, he and his brother Derald,
also a psychologist, had done studies and writing on Asian American psychology, and their work was considered seminal in the field. At the reception
following his talk, Dr. Sue related a story to a few of us chatting with him
informally, the gist of which remains with me to this day. He said his father,
an immigrant from China, still didn't seem to understand just what it was
that his son was doing. It didn't seem to matter that Stanley had a doctorate
and a very good job at a well-known educational institution, that he was a
published author, or that he was often called upon to speak in public. His
father still sometimes wondered when Stanley was going to get a real job.
This story brought smiles of understanding and recognition to some of us
standing around him. In my mind I was finishing the sentence with ". . . a real
job in a real science, like a medical doctor or a physicist or a chemist or an
engineer. Something where you can make a decent living."

When I was at the UC Berkeley clinic, we had just two other Asian
American therapists and one African American clinician. But the word was
out not only to us but to all nooks and crannies of the institution that the
staff and faculty needed to diversify to keep up with the diversity of the
student body. Our staff was not opposed to this idea, but openings for new

blood were rare since, once hired, people tended to stay. Getting new money for new staff was typically an uphill battle—tantamount to getting approval from the United Nations or requesting permission to build a nuclear reactor.

The most active and encouraging tool our clinic had to recruit diverse, fresh faces was through our post-doctoral and post-MSW (master of social work) clinical internship training program. Through a rigorous vetting process, we were able to select between three and five interns each year who would become part of our staff for that academic year. In return for their service, the program would offer them ongoing clinical seminars and close supervision of their clients. Through this program we were able to select well-prepared interns of all stripes, from the typical categories of people of color to those identifying as LGBTQ or "queer," as many on campus preferred to be identified. On the rare occasion when we had an opening for a new staff member, these former interns gave us a readymade pool of applicants to turn to.

By the time I retired from the working world and took my leave of colleagues and the students I had grown so fond of, I was comforted to know that I was leaving a profession that had changed its look in my own lifetime. When I first started doing therapy, most of the other Asian American therapists were found on the West Coast, with a sprinkling on the East Coast. The number was small, and if we didn't all know each other personally, we had at least heard each other's names. It wasn't difficult to keep up with the literature on Asian American psychology, though new research and writing was appearing at a rapid pace.

Today, forty years later, I am happy to report that much has changed. The number of Asian American clinicians has grown at a fairly steady pace, and now there are far too many names to keep track of. New research on Asian American psychology, written by Asian American psychologists of different ethnicities, continues to enter the field. And it seems that talking about all the details of one's life to a perfect stranger is now understood as the accepted mode of treatment.

All this would indicate that in this rather strange, very Western tradition of healing, I am now far from the one and only Asian American practitioner.

6

CROSSING OVER

I still have the picture, preserved in its plastic sleeve and filed away with all the other treasures in my permanent file. I first happened upon it years ago while casually leafing through a magazine in the waiting room of my doctor's office. When I turned the page and came to the picture, I stopped short. I couldn't stop staring at it; I wanted that picture. So I confess, when no one was looking, I surreptitiously tore it out of the magazine, leaving an annoying hole in the story it belonged to. It felt like an act I did not fully control. All I knew was that I had to have that picture. It wasn't easy to tear a full-page picture from a large *Life* magazine without attracting attention.

Though I don't approve of such thievery, it would be far from true to say I am sorry I took it, since even now, decades later, I find myself going to my file cabinet, taking out the picture, and just staring at it for a moment. Staring and wondering and remembering all over again.

It's a picture of two children on their way to school. They live in a small village in the rainforest outside Bogotá, Colombia. Every morning, in order to get to their school, they must cross a canyon half a mile wide and 400 yards deep. To make this crossing, the nine-year-old girl hooks herself and a large jute bag secured across her body to a pulley; inside the bag is her five-year-old brother, too young to make the crossing on his own. Standing at the edge of the canyon, the girl—her name, the caption says, is Daisy—slight and slender, hugs the bag to her body. With her free hand she grasps a heavy wooden branch shaped like a V and makes sure it is solidly in place over a steel cable. The cable is firmly anchored to a spot on the other side of the canyon. Daisy takes a deep breath and shoves off. Her feet dangling, hand clutching the branch tightly, she and her brother whiz across the gaping canyon below. In the picture of them midair, her face is surprisingly composed. One minute later, the pair touch down on the other side and proceed to school.

No matter how often I look at this picture, it takes my breath away. Sometimes it's just what it is, a picture of two children getting to school by using extreme measures. At other times when I look at it, I have only questions, questions about those children *after* they get to school: Why is school so important to them? When they're there, do they experience the magic of learning, the excitement of numbers, words, books, maps? The mysteries introduced and then unveiled? When they get home after school, what do they do with their newfound knowledge? Who do they talk to; what do they talk about; how do they cope with the routine of their lives? Now, so many years later, what has become of their lives? I want to look Daisy, now a young woman, in the eyes and ask: Was it worth the trip, that sixty-second journey fraught with peril each time she pushed off?

• • •

World War II, raging across Europe, finally came to US shores when Japan bombed Pearl Harbor on December 7, 1941, the "day that will live in infamy." In response, President Franklin D. Roosevelt declared war on Japan, and the United States was officially engaged in World War II. Ironically, one of Roosevelt's first official wartime acts was targeted against his own citizens: in February 1942, he issued Executive Order 9066 ordering the removal of all persons of Japanese ancestry—American-born citizens as well as the immigrant population of Issei, the first-generation "aliens"—from the entire West Coast. This area, extending from Washington to the border with Mexico, was deemed a "security risk," and no Japanese American could be trusted to live there. I have heard and read about the immediate anti-Japanese hysteria that ensued and some of the outrageous stories of espionage attributed to Japanese Americans. One such fantastic tale was of Japanese American farmers planting crops in the shape of arrows pointing the way to—what? (One rumor was to munitions dumps or other "sensitive" facilities.) For all the tall tales circulating, in the end, cases of Japanese Americans spying for the enemy were so rare as to be nearly nonexistent; in fact, some Japanese American soldiers ended up working for American military intelligence, translating messages intercepted from the Japanese military.

But first, the hysteria of war prevailed, and the forced removal and incarceration of Japanese Americans came off without much protest and with little resistance from anyone. The majority of the Japanese Americans, between 110,000 and 120,000 men, women, and children of all ages, were shipped off to hastily constructed camps in the western and southern parts of the country: the mountains, deserts, and swamplands of Utah, Idaho, Colorado, Wyoming, Arizona, California, and Arkansas.

When I try to imagine the mere logistics of such a move, I find the process mind-boggling. The myriad steps required to suddenly and with little warning move 120,000 people from their comfortable homes into makeshift housing in faraway camps constituted a monumental task. The Japanese Americans had to be informed of the forced removal; barracks-style living quarters had to be constructed practically overnight; trains were needed to quietly transport the prisoners to their camps; armed soldiers were enlisted to stand guard and help with the forced removal at train stations or wherever crowds of those removed gathered. It all made the panic and fear of an entire country stand out in stunning relief.

Of course, it was easy to locate the people to remove because they looked more "foreign" than the average white American: they were darker-skinned with black hair, had different-shaped eyes and faces, tended to be shorter and smaller, and had unpronounceable names like Nakamura and Suzuki. In urban communities, they tended to live together and had businesses that were often quite successful; in the country, they had flourishing farms and gardens. But that all simply magnified the threat: they were moving up and into other communities in cities and farmlands—soon they would take over everything. They were fast becoming "the yellow peril."

It's strange to think of my parents—mild-mannered, cooperative, thoughtful and intelligent, hardworking—as a yellow peril. But they were living in coastal Seattle and so were forced to leave, like everyone else in their building and neighborhood—though they didn't go to the camps with everyone else. They went to Wyoming.

Before my parents left Seattle, their friends, many of whom lived in the same apartment building, tried hard to convince them not to go to Wyoming but to go with them to the camp. They reasoned that it was better to stick together—better for their spirits, safer for their bodies. But Dad could not be moved from his decision. In that horrible moment he was lucky enough to have a choice, and he chose not to raise his child in a concentration camp.

My parents' Seattle friends were right about one thing: those 120,000 people stuck together in ten camps across the country did have each other. They had each other in the blocks and blocks of barracks-style housing constructed for them in every one of the ten camps. They had each other in the communal bathrooms and latrines, often located far from their barracks apartments; they had each other in the mess halls where everyone had to go to eat and where families were often separated from each other, the mothers and children eating at different times than the fathers; they had each other in the conversations families and couples had that were meant only for one another; they had each other when couples wanted to satisfy their desires for sexual intimacy. Each barracks building, with its one thin, shared wall separating one apartment from the next, made privacy a thing of the past, a whisper of memory or maybe a figment of the imagination.

My dad could not have known any of these details before his friends and all the others had actually arrived at their destinations; the incarcerees didn't even know where they were going or what it would be like until they got there. So Dad either had a vivid imagination, or he was prescient.

Rural Wyoming could not have been a bigger contrast to the crowded barracks life of the incarceration camps. I was born in Sheridan the year after my parents and sister arrived there. To my knowledge, there weren't many Japanese Americans living in or around Sheridan. And probably because of this, my grandparents had been able to make a comfortable life there. They were well-respected members of the town, a town of farmers and hunters and cowboys. Grandma and Grandpa made their contribution by growing vegetables for the locals. They had developed a following; they posed no threat—until the war. Until suddenly, out of nowhere, the congenial, vegetable-raising couple was joined by three people who had been banished from their homes for their suspicious appearance, and then it became apparent that the old couple looked like those questionable new arrivals and like the enemy we were fighting in Asia.

When Dad moved his family back to Sheridan, he went to merchants and other people he'd known as a kid, thinking someone would hire him in their store or business establishment. He had gone to school there, had been an athlete and a good student. His job search turned out to be futile; no one would hire him. Grandpa was also feeling the repercussions of the war in Asia: he had been asked to leave the Rotary Club because the other members thought "it would be better for him." That excuse or some form of it was code for what Dad and Mom had seen and heard on the West Coast in more explicit terms: "Japs" were "not welcome," not in stores, not in neighborhoods, not in schools or the workplace. "Japs" needed to "go home," back to "where they came from." My parents knew what "better for them/him/her" meant. That's why they were in Sheridan, Wyoming, and their friends were in incarceration camps.

Our family—my parents, now both my sister and myself, and my grandparents—didn't stay in Wyoming for long. Sugar was in especially short supply, and rationing was happening at home and in Europe. That put sugar beets in high demand, and the US government had begun leasing farmland to families willing to move to Montana to grow foodstuffs for the war effort. They had even begun to release a slow trickle of Japanese Americans from some of the incarceration camps to help grow beets and also wheat. Dad decided this would be a good move for him since, as a farmer, he could be his own boss. He must have known it wouldn't be easy—he would be going there alone, without any relatives to help him with the farm, and he would have young children to provide for. But at least he wouldn't be stuck looking for a job in a small town where people didn't want him.

There is nothing like the broad eastern plains of Montana to remind you of your place in the universe; human beings are just one small speck on the face of the earth. This is where we landed, on a small farm surrounded by the rolling hills, buttes, mesas, and flatlands that stretch out to the distant horizon and beyond, to places we have all heard of—New York, Paris, Shanghai. We can only trust that those cities are out there because from our farmhouse in the middle of nowhere, there was no indication that anything else in the world existed.

We moved into a rundown, too-small-for-our-family house on a small patch of land about ten miles outside Hardin. A number of Japanese American farmers in the valley had children, but actually getting together was the challenging part. Not everyone had a telephone, and while I'm not sure how our mothers communicated, sometimes we did get together with other kids. I remember that when a mom and her kids came to visit, the visits seemed like pretty formal occasions. Our mothers would sit and talk over tea and cookies. We kids would roam the farmyard or ride tricycles or climb trees or generally explore the countryside. We could fill our water pistols from any of the small rivulets of water running through the pasture and have cooling shootouts on a hot summer day. Or we might play cowboys and Indians like we saw in the movies (nobody wanted to be an Indian), shooting our pistols, "six-shooters" loaded with paper caps. When we pulled the trigger, the hammer of the pistol would land on the paper cap, which was designed to pop when hit hard enough. That was enough to satisfy us. Eventually, we'd get thirsty and head back to the house for Kool-Aid in electric colors—lime, cherry, lemon—and some store-bought cookies or maybe some homemade treats, cake or cookies made by our mom or the visiting mom. In Japanese culture, you never went to someone's home empty-handed, and guests were always offered something to eat and drink. After a while, the mom reined in her kids and they all went home, and for a short time afterward the house and yard would feel eerily quiet.

The reverse would also happen: Mom would take us to someone else's farm, and we would repeat the ritual there. Sometimes we'd visit a family who had a horse or two, and we'd get to take turns riding them. This was heaven for us since we didn't have a horse of our own. We would ride until our legs were stiff and ached from the unfamiliar position of being stretched out trying to straddle a large, rounded belly. That night at home, sore but happy, we'd dream of being in our cowgirl hats and boots, tearing across the prairie on beautiful palomino ponies just like Roy Rogers on Trigger.

We didn't have horses, but we had other animals to take care of. We had chickens that would let us rob the eggs right out from under them if we didn't want to make a second trip to the coop later that day; mean-tempered geese that might decide to come at us with wings outspread, mouths open and hissing; and turkeys so timid they would sit down, close their eyes, and stay stock-still if they felt scared. We could stroke their red combs and believe the story we had heard, that turkeys were so stupid that if it started to rain, they would look up to see what was happening and drown because they wouldn't look down again. All of us girls learned to milk a cow, but we left that daily task to our oldest sister; instead, my younger sister and I fed cute orphan lambs Pepsi Cola bottles full of cow's milk, topped with a rubber nipple.

School was the other place we kids found the most human contact outside our family. But a one-room country schoolhouse with under twenty kids was not exactly a social beehive. To limit things even further, these fewer than twenty kids spanned all six grades of elementary school. Our ages ranged from six to thirteen. Trying to find one best girlfriend among such a small and limited group happened only with a little luck. But I did get lucky. My best friend was Beverly, and even though she was not in my grade—she was slightly older—that was close enough, and we became good friends and did almost everything together. On some days we even swapped lunches. Poor Beverly. She never complained about my single slice of bologna slapped between two slices of squishy white bread held together with a veneer of mayonnaise. Sometimes I added a thin slice of soft, alarmingly yellow cheese. I know exactly what went into my sandwiches because I made them myself. I don't remember what I got in return, but there is no question in my mind that Beverly got the short end of that stick. I can still see her curly blond hair and her glasses, and now when I think of her, I remember her kindness. She was never mean the way girls can be sometimes, and I remember her as a good student. She had an older sister and a younger male cousin at the school, and I liked them all.

During recess we played baseball, with our teacher often pitching so the smaller younger kids—that included me—would have a fair chance at hitting the ball. We also played tag and took turns riding a bike if someone had brought one to school.

School was our world away from home, and I loved going there. I loved learning what we were taught in my grade, but I also got to listen to what was going on in the other grades, and what I took in from that exposure served me well later on. Our teacher, Mrs. Jenkins, was tireless, teaching us the basic three Rs along with music and art. She was neither a musician nor an artist, but she found art projects she could manage to teach us so in the end we would all have an art piece to take home or display at school. She ordered children's musical instruments from a catalog, and when they arrived in the mail, we all gathered round to see what instruments emerged from the box. We could try them out—I remember plastic flutes, triangles, a xylophone—and find one that seemed to suit our personalities. She did her best to teach us how to play them. And, as I said, she was our star baseball pitcher on the playground. She cleaned the schoolhouse at the end of the day, and in the harsh winter months she stoked the coal-burning stove and placed on top of it a pot of canned soup so every child could have a bowl for lunch. Mrs. Jenkins was remarkable, a marvel of organization and discipline and energy. Her dedication made everything work.

My other education came from looking at *Life* magazine. We always had it on our coffee table at home, the current issue along with a few back issues, and it is a happy and stable memory of my childhood. Looking at it every week was like being in a parallel universe. I especially loved the pictures of far-off places: the exciting hustle and bustle on the streets of New York or San Francisco; their exact opposite in the serene temples in China and Japan; the mysterious Eiffel Tower in Paris or the London Bridge (why did we sing it was "falling down" when it wasn't at all?); the painted natives in "deepest, darkest Africa;" the mother kangaroos in Australia with babies' heads sticking out of their stomach pouches.

It was also *Life* that made me think about what kind of work there was to do in the world: doctors saving lives at home but also far away in needy, often dangerous places, which made it seem even more exciting; scientists in lab coats squinting into microscopes, ready to make a new discovery; photographers able to travel anywhere to get pictures of anything; teachers who could teach anywhere in the world. All of them, their lives romanticized through the lens of the *Life* photographer.

All those captivating pictures whetted my appetite. I wanted to see the people and places for myself. Someday, I told myself, I would go. Someday, I would leave the farm.

And suddenly it happened: we found ourselves packing up for a move to Denver, Colorado. Farming was not paying off, so Dad was getting out while the getting was still good, while he still had the time and energy to start over and take care of his family. We chose Denver because my mother's family was there, her mother and most of her brothers and sisters. We would not be alone; for the first time ever, we could have a community not only of real aunties and uncles and cousins but also of other Japanese Americans, and maybe it would grow bigger after we were there for awhile.

I was both excited and nervous. It seemed odd to suddenly get what I had dreamed of.

• • •

It was the mid-1950s when we got to Denver, an emblematic time for America as well as for me since I would be entering junior high in my new school in the big city.

Looking around, a time-traveler going back to the 1950s would see a nation in the white heat of growth and development. It seemed like America couldn't be stopped. The war was over, and the country was on a roll. Everywhere we looked we could see bright-faced, exuberant Americans, consuming all the new and wonderful products rolling off production lines and into the kitchens and living rooms of brand-new homes. My mother never voiced it aloud, but I wondered if she secretly longed for one of those pale pink or avocado-green stoves and matching refrigerators showcased in the home-furnishing magazines; we made do with the old, standard white models we brought with us from the farm. The furniture stores showed shiny wooden dining room tables big enough to seat a large and growing family, living room couches with matching chairs. A future president of the United States, in his Hollywood career phase, was advertising the latest wrinkle-proof, no-iron men's shirt, while streamlined, fashion-heavy automobiles were turning up in showrooms across the country. We had seen a few of those cars in the yards of well-off farmers right about the time we left Hardin. A motto of the time was "better living through chemistry." I liked the sound of it; it sounded so futuristic, so smart. Life seemed full of promise and opportunity and wealth to be acquired by all. It looked like everybody was enjoying a boom time, big-time.

It was also the era of John Wayne—the "Duke," the two-fisted hero and icon of rugged American individualism. The Duke set the standard for all the cowboy and Indian movies coming out of Hollywood, some of which we had seen before we left Montana. He wasn't in every movie, but all the cowboys acted tough and stoic like he did, and the plots were always the same: the cowboys are trapped somewhere and outnumbered by a large and savage group of howling, half-naked, painted Indians waving tomahawks in the air, shooting arrows, and closing in on their innocent victims. (Nothing like the Indians we saw in Hardin.) Just as the savages are ready to descend on them for the slaughter, off in the distance we hear the strain of bugles.

Then, their horses galloping full speed onto the screen, bugles blaring, brass buttons gleaming against their deep blue jackets, the American flag hoisted high and waving boldly in the wind—the cavalry! The Indians are routed! The day is saved! The audience cheers and claps.

Along with those images of cowboys and Indians, I was also aware of the enduring Asian movie figures Charlie Chan and Fu Manchu. (They had not been as popular in Montana as the cowboys and Indians.) Both were played by white men made up to look like they were Chinese. Fu Manchu—Dr. Fu Manchu—was evil incarnate with a scrawny moustache, a long, thin tendril on each side of his upper lip hanging down well past his chin. He would stroke his moustache with long, slender fingers and stare directly ahead with cold, unblinking eyes, letting us know that he was master-minding some fiendish, horrible, destructive plot. Americans no longer had the yellow peril of Japan threatening our doors; we now had a new yellow peril: the devilish, "inscrutable" Fu Manchu.

Charlie Chan was slightly more ambiguous since he was a good guy, a detective on the right side of the law—but still not exactly respected and usually portrayed as ingratiating, not very manly, and thus unthreatening. Off to the side, his "Number One Son," portrayed by an actual Asian man, was even more unassuming and could appear stupid. I have read that the early Charlie Chan movies, when the detective was played by an Asian actor, never really took off. It was only when the star was a white man made up to look Asian that the movies became box office successes.

A few years later, when we were high school seniors, my girlfriends and I fell in love with the movie *Breakfast at Tiffany's* and the winsome, pixie-like Audrey Hepburn, a relative newcomer to the movies. I noticed but brushed aside Mickey Rooney, playing Mr. Yunioshi, a Japanese tenant who lived in the same building as Audrey Hepburn. He was made up to look the way most Asian men were thought of at that time: short and squat with buck teeth and round, Coke-bottle–thick eyeglasses sliding down a nose with a bridge too flat to hold them up. When provoked, he would admonish Audrey Hepburn, playing Holly Golightly, by yelling "Miss Go-rite-ry!" This character did nothing to enhance the plot of the movie; he was there strictly to be laughed at. I knew the stereotype but tried to ignore it.

Asian women, in contrast, all became Suzie Wong in the eyes of the movie-watching public. About the same time my high school friends and I were falling in love with Audrey Hepburn, William Holden in another movie was falling in love with Suzie Wong, a sexy, beautiful Chinese prostitute. The movie was a hit, as had been an earlier Broadway play version. Suzie was played by an actress who was half Asian and half white, which helped cement the role and image of Asian women as prostitutes in the public's consciousness. The other standard role for an Asian woman was as a maid in a big mansion owned by a wealthy white businessman. Actresses in this role were barely noticed and were on screen for only minutes. The two roles—the barely visible, submissive maid or the hot and sexy prostitute—gave me little choice for positive self-reflection, so, like my friends, I stuck with Audrey Hepburn. At least she left room for dreaming and imagining.

If anyone recognized these attitudes and images as a shadow side of the times, of that booming, wealthy decade the 1950s, no one mentioned it openly. I certainly didn't. When I was entering junior high in Denver, all I wanted was to be like everyone else: to have friends, to have a good time, to do well in school. To fit in.

But it wasn't easy to be like everyone else. I had just moved from a one-room schoolhouse in isolated rural Montana and was entering a junior high of several hundred students in a big city in a different state. When I set foot in my new "home room," it seemed like crossing state borders was going to be the easiest part of this move.

The dean of girls at the school, a short, soft-spoken woman, ushered me into the classroom and introduced me to the teacher, who then drew the attention of the class and introduced me to the sea of white faces seated before me. I had never seen so many white kids all together in one room. I was stunned, and in that moment I wished I could click together the heels of my ruby-red shoes and, like Dorothy in the *Wizard of Oz*, get whisked back to, in my case, Montana. But it was too late; there was no turning back. Terrified, I managed a weak smile, and to my surprise, it seemed like everyone smiled back.

Those first few months, as I nervously took in the scene of my new junior high, it looked to me like all my peers were white, well-off, and well-dressed in the latest junior high fashion. The girls wore skirts and angora sweaters, saddle shoes or white bucks, and socks that matched the color of their sweaters; the boys wore khaki pants, madras shirts, and saddle shoes or white bucks. Sometimes the boys wore Levi jeans and polo shirts, and the girls wore sweaters that weren't angora and socks that didn't match the color of their sweaters, but whatever the outfit, it was stylish and well thought-out. It must have been in the spring, when the weather warmed up, that the girls suddenly appeared in stiffly starched crinoline petticoats that puffed out their skirts like antebellum hoop skirts.

But even more intimidating than their appearance was the fact that they were smart. And verbal. And loquacious. They could talk about everything, from world events like the Sputnik space launch to movies, makeup, and sports. And to my never-ending amazement, no one seemed the least bit hesitant to speak out in the classroom. In fact, they seemed to want to speak out. They liked to speak out. At the first opportunity to answer a question, a forest of arms would shoot into the air and wave back and forth like branches swayed by a strong breeze. The student called on would give an answer—sometimes factual, sometimes a comment or an opinion that was meant to provoke or challenge the rest of us. These students loved engaging in friendly competition with each other, both verbally and on written tests. Some friends openly compared their test scores to see whose was higher. Eventually, we all found out without much effort who had gotten the best grade on the test, whatever the subject. I loved the mental stimulation but never felt compelled to try to compete with any of these über-students. I just tried to keep up; I'd never seen anything like this.

In fact, I never felt compelled to compete much with anyone. Competition wasn't something I'd had much experience with. It was too tied in to Japanese cultural norms that frowned on bringing attention to oneself. In my socially traditional Japanese family, such behavior was considered rude and unacceptable. My parents had imbued us, their children and representatives in the world at large, with appropriate Japanese behavior: no one talked excessively, no one raised her voice, no one ever asked to be the center of attention, no one felt her remarks were so interesting or important that they had to be trumpeted, and certainly no one ever crowded out anyone else to be heard. In traditional social behavior, the other person was deferred to, and because she knew this, there was no need for competition or vying for attention. Each person knew her turn would come; each person behaved according to rules both parties understood. This mutual understanding made for smooth, well-modulated, well-mannered social interactions.

Even though we kids didn't get many chances to practice our good Japanese manners among other Japanese Americans, since we still hadn't met many even in Denver, those manners are probably what helped me get through junior high and senior high school without any major social or academic dramas. I tried my best to keep up with my fellow students, but I didn't think of ways to try to best them. I wasn't perceived as a threat. I was seen as shy and quiet and probably naive. I now understand that what was happening was more sinister: what began as a cultural norm morphed into my underlying belief that I was not, and couldn't be, as good as my white counterparts. I couldn't talk as fast or speak out as quickly or with as much confidence as they could. Yet I knew that if I wanted to succeed in school, I would have to at least try to speak up, to join the discussion. But I found it nearly impossible to squeeze my way into the verbal scrimmage of my competitive classmates. If I saw an opening, I was always a beat behind and so ended up letting yet another discussion pass me by. When I was finally quick enough to raise my hand and be called on, it was mortifying to have all eyes in the room turn to me to hear what smart answer I was going to contribute. I was terrified of sounding stupid or like I was repeating something already said or talking about something discussed two questions ago. My teachers, for many semesters, sent home report cards telling my parents that I was a good student—but "she doesn't speak up enough in class," "she needs to participate more in class discussions."

That did seem like the passport to success—learning how to talk, which meant learning how to verbalize *everything*, everything that was observed, experienced, thought about, and felt. As I said, my classmates loved speaking out in the classroom. But when it came to talking about other things besides the metaphors in the poem assigned for English or the latest impossible math assignment or the test coming up in Colorado history, they were just as talkative. They talked openly about their weekend ski trips: where the best spot was and how they got there—the train to Winter Park, driving with family or a friend with a car to A Basin, Breckenridge, or Loveland, places I'd never heard of—the hardest to get to, the best powder, the best ski lifts, the most recently tested skis, boots, and bindings. All in a jargon I would soon become familiar with even if I never made it to the slopes. They talked and acted like they expected to ski with the best equipment; dress in the latest, warmest, most weatherproof ski clothes; and go on family vacations, from camping in state parks to flying to New York or California. Most astounding of all, they expected to be seen and heard.

Junior high is the age of raging hormones, so every chance they got, the girls talked about boys and what to do to attract them and how to come in contact with them. They talked about appearance—clothes, hairdos, hips and thighs that were too ample or the opposite, uncooperative parents, places to go for fun, who had the last party, and who all was there. All this lay far outside my realm of experience, and I felt lost and befuddled.

What I did learn quickly was to use my quiet and shy persona to my advantage. I remained quiet and watched carefully, observing and listening to everything with a new intent. It was like having to learn another language or the rules for a game I'd only heard about but now had to learn how to play.

In the girls' bathroom, in the halls, outside on the school grounds, I paid close attention. I giggled along with the rest of the girls when Linda described how awkward her Saturday morning dance class was, with the boys not wanting to dance with the girls and the girls hoping they would get partnered with the right boy and not some scrawny nerd. (Ballroom dance class? Really? That was a first for me.) I listened for language—what slang expressions were used and when. When something was good, it was "really neat": a neat thing happened, a neat new piece of sports equipment, a neat place to go. I studied the *way* hip junior high kids said things. There was a certain style to what was said—a kind of teasing humor, a friendly tension especially among the boys, who would often rib each other with clever put-downs that were clearly "guy" jokes about somehow not measuring up academically, athletically, socially—nothing seemed off limits. Yet no one seemed to take offense.

I watched for body language and facial expressions as the girls joked and teased and gossiped about other girls and about boys. Giggling and conspiratorial glances, someone who had actually gone on a date—her parents let her go even if she wasn't yet in high school. And it wasn't a group date, it was just the two of them. And, of course, I observed the clothes, who wore what—the cool kids versus the nerds versus the tougher kids from neighborhoods farther away. One day I learned that something as simple as a turned-up blouse collar gave the impression that I was a little tougher than I actually was (or wanted to be), and a new friend quickly turned mine back down. And lipstick was definitely out of the question before the eighth grade, unless you were one of those girls who kept her collar turned up!

It took a little more time for me to even recognize the existence of the separate and specific social circles so many of my classmates belonged to. The younger girls would listen closely to the older girls as they began talking about their futures in high school: their coming-out parties and debutante balls, primarily for the Anglo girls; being "tapped" for a high school sorority or "riding club," separate ones for Anglo girls and Jewish girls; separate religious youth groups for Anglos and Jews. I had so much to learn.

The more I took in, the more I wondered where I belonged. I didn't seem to fit in comfortably in any specific group. I had never met anyone Jewish before junior high school, but I soon learned the meaning of words like synagogue, menorah, and Hanukkah and their importance to my many classmates who came from Jewish backgrounds. Some came from families who were very liberal in their religious and social practices; others were from families who practiced their religion more strictly. I was learning to make distinctions among my friends. Other friends came from families who were considered "old Denver" families, meaning they had taste and manners and "old money." My family was struggling working class, but because of the elevated value we placed on education, I seemed to be making friends with the kids who clearly came from much better-off, middle-class families. Our values, goals, and aspirations weren't all that different. It was the financial gap that separated us.

Well, that and some of the social behaviors that only my siblings and I noticed. As the minority in every sense, it was up to us to learn the ways of the mainstream. I clearly remember the shock and confusion I experienced the first time a friend offered me a cookie. We were having lunch together at school, and she offered me one of the cookies on her lunch tray. I dutifully and automatically responded with the manners I had learned at home from the time I was able to learn: I politely refused, waiting to be coaxed until I finally gave in and took one. But my friend, taking me at my word, took a cookie for herself and put the rest aside. I thought this was round one and that clearly our little drama was unfinished. She would come back with the cookies and insist that I have one; only then could I comply. But for her, that was the end of it—she had offered and then taken her own cookie. I could tell she wasn't being rude, so this must be the way things were done. It took a few more times of testing the rules and ending up deprived until I eventually learned to accept something the first time it was offered, as that was likely to be the last time.

Switching between the two worlds—the modest, contained, and predictable world of home and extended family and the loud, brash, swaggering world of school, peers, and friends—was a tiring proposition. Being with family or extended family was not much work, but being in the world "out there" demanded constant attention to self, to others, and to the details of human interaction. I have described what I had to do to make it at my new junior high in Denver, in fact, what I had to do to make it in the white world, the Copernicus axiom: I had to see myself as the center of the universe—the sun—and see everyone else as revolving around me like planets. In Western culture, I learned, the individual was what counted and every action, beginning at birth, was geared toward developing and shaping that individual into his or her own sun. In my family's world, a person was taught always to consider the needs and expectations of the larger group and to understand that that group was as important as any single individual, if not more important. For my Japanese parents, being the center of the universe was a heretical idea, fostering selfish and uncouth behavior. For us kids, learning how to act Copernican felt at best uncomfortable, at worst, like something we might never fully achieve. But we had no choice. Once outside the house, we did our best to maneuver in a world of differences and indifferences, to fit in, to look out for ourselves first and foremost, to be noticed, to act like we deserved to be seen and heard, to compete for success. To show that we mattered.

• • •

Those days of trying to find my way in a new city and in a new, large junior high school are long past, and sometimes, when I look back, I do wonder how my siblings and I made it through school, college, and on to jobs to become fully functioning, contributing members of the society at large. I know of one or two people who didn't make it, and all one has to do is watch the nightly news to hear about people the world over who are losing the struggle to find that better life and some who are losing the struggle merely to survive.

There is an overarching story I can tell as to why my life turned out as it has. It's not a complicated story, and it is not filled with drama and heroics.

My parents were hardworking and wanted to give their children the best life possible. Our family life was stable, and while we were decidedly poor and there was never anything "extra," we also never went hungry, lacked clothing, or had moments without shelter. As I have said before, my family's values were in sync with the mainstream middle-class values of the time, so education and family relationships were paramount. As a result, my parents made sure that all their children went to excellent public schools. While there, I made some good and lasting friendships. When I left for college or for any of the other reasons that kept me roaming—a new job across the country, going to grad school, or trying a new adventure—I knew without asking that if I needed to, I could always return home where I would be safe, fed, and welcome to stay as long as I needed. I didn't plan all this. I was just lucky to have the family and the circumstances that allowed for this security.

• • •

It has been over a decade since I first saw the picture of those children in *Life* magazine: Daisy dangling from the cable, clutching the tree branch, her brother tucked inside the jute bag she holds close to her. They are whizzing across the deep canyon risking everything to get to the other side, to get to school, to make better lives for themselves. Today, these two would no longer be children; they are young adults. I long to know where they are now and what they are doing. Are they realizing the hopes and dreams they had for themselves? Are there moments that make them regret they ever made the crossing? Would I dare to chance telling them my own story of having to cross over to another world? Would they understand or think me impertinent to even dare to make the comparison?

But alas, theirs is a story I am left only to imagine, to make up my own version of what their lives have been and might be today. The mystery of it all sometimes leaves me wondering whether for Daisy and her brother, the crossing itself was not the safest, surest part of their journey.

7

SAINTS AND SINNERS

There is nothing like music or a song to bring light to a darkened memory, to fill an empty gap. One day, when I'd finally had it with all the bad news coming at me from my car radio—violence, wars, killing, more violence, more wars, more killing—I switched to KCSM, the Bay-area jazz station, a welcome relief to my jangled nerves as I made my way across town to visit a friend. In that disgruntled moment, I tuned in to the sounds of a fantastic piano player whose name I never caught who was playing like a maniac, pounding the ivories, propelling his hands across the keys from treble to bass and back again, making every key pay its due. The sound was electric, exciting, alive. He was terrific.

Listening to that high-octane, creative energy sent me back to a time when I was young, going with friends to hear a lot of live jazz at small Black jazz clubs in Philadelphia. That was decades ago, in the mid-1960s, but was that ever a time for jazz! Great jazz musicians were everywhere, playing local gigs, playing in mostly Black clubs in the big cities, and playing with each other whenever and wherever they had the chance. In Philly, we knew that when we left the club after a show they would still be there, jamming with each other until the wee hours of the morning.

But I hadn't always listened to jazz, hadn't grown up with it like the kids in that Philly neighborhood back in the mid-1960s. In fact, Philly was where I was introduced to what seemed to me new, far-out, "bohemian" music that was mostly associated with Black musicians, Black people in general, and maybe also with the beat generation and other sophisticated artist types—all of whom smoked (often more than just cigarettes), drank mostly alcoholic beverages, and sat around reciting poetry. Not that I would have minded it, that calculated, artsy image, but I had never identified myself that way. No, I just count myself lucky to have been in the right place at the right time to be exposed to this music, which I have grown to appreciate even more over time, in the broader scheme of life and music.

I just happened to have landed in Philadelphia as a VISTA volunteer. In the 1960s, VISTA, or Volunteers in Service to America, was still a very new federal program, an idealistic scheme created by an idealistic government, initially formulated by an idealistic, idealized, youthful president to, simply put, fight poverty. It was perfect for the young and hopeful generation of new college graduates or students still in college who wanted a real-world break from their studies. It was not quite as exotic or risky as the Peace Corps, the other, better-known vision of President John F. Kennedy, since all the service would take place within the United States and its territories. No foreign placements, unless someone from New York City felt that working in Georgia or Arizona was like being in a foreign country.

So after finishing college and graduating with a degree in English, at the time a degree not suited for much in the practical world, I told my parents I had decided to join VISTA. After learning that it was a volunteer organization and that I would be paid only a small stipend at the end of my year of service, my father, typically a man of few words and not one to express much emotion, to my surprise conveyed his disapproval of this decision. He didn't yell at me or raise his voice or make a scene. But he did have a sit-down talk with me, telling me in a tone more frustrated than angry that he couldn't understand why I would spend four years in college, work hard for a degree, go into debt to get it, and then go off to some poverty-stricken neighborhood someplace and work for nothing. In retrospect, I realize he was asking himself why, after all the years in which he had been working to get his family *out* of poverty, I would *choose* to go back into it and not be paid at all. I told him that it was a chance for me to do something useful in life, that since it was a government program I could put off paying my student loans for another year, that it was my decision—and that I was going to do it anyway, regardless of whether he approved. He didn't say he wouldn't let me go, but he made his feelings known, and I confess that when I left for Philadelphia, I felt sad and uneasy that I was leaving without his approval. I wonder now if a small part of Dad might have liked that I'd had enough spunk to stand up to him. I'm not sure how I managed it, as that was not the way kids from a good Japanese family spoke to a parent.

VISTA in those days was not that well organized; it seemed like a good program still trying to find its legs. So when I landed in Philly, it wasn't exactly clear what I would be doing. Some designated neighborhood service agencies had requested volunteers or agreed to take them, and some staff in these agencies would function as on-site trainers and mentors. They would steer volunteers to the programs where they felt we would either best fit in or be most needed. I was assigned to St. Martha's Settlement House in South Philadelphia. St. Martha's, although it retained the old-fashioned title of "settlement house," was actually functioning more like a community center, providing free services mostly to neighborhood youth. When I arrived I found that maybe five volunteers were already there, trying to make inroads into and expand upon some of the projects sponsored by St. Martha's. Before my year was over, there would be close to a dozen of us, though the numbers would fluctuate as new blood arrived and those whose year of service had ended left. There were usually more women than men.

South Philly was unambiguous about its racial divide. Eighth Street was a main drag through the district, and it handily separated the African American section from the Italian American section. There didn't seem to be much crossover between the two sides. In that sense, Eighth Street might as well have been a river. I can happily state that there was no violence between the two sides the year I was there, and even though St. Martha's was on the Black side of Eighth Street and overwhelmingly served the Black population, some of its staff were neighborhood Italians. There appeared to be no open, hostile enmity, just no mixing or mingling.

In my early days at St. Martha's, when I was brand new, I remember feeling my own tension, wondering if things would get strained enough for some little spark to ignite a frayed nerve lying just under the surface and set us off and running into a full-blown riot. I arrived in late summer and the heat felt nearly unbearable—a heavy, humid, urban, East Coast heat that enveloped my body, weighing it down, making me damp and clammy from the burden of slogging my way through it. I thought I knew heat, coming from Colorado. That was a dry heat that could feel like it was searing your skin, but this, this wet heat, was something entirely different. I could hear in my head that popular Judy Collins folk song about a riot happening in a city "in the heat of the summer, when the pavements were burning." I had never really understood that song until I landed on the streets of South Philadelphia. It seemed to me now that the heat made everything about life in South Philly feel more tenuous and volatile.

Both neighborhoods, the Italian and the Black, were composed of narrow, uneven cobblestone streets lined by narrow brick row houses with adjoining walls, some up to three stories high. This made both sides dense with people of all ages and especially with kids of all ages on the Black side. A stroll through the Italian side revealed a community proud of its heritage and its neighborhood. The brick row houses were well maintained, some of them showing the tediously applied outline around every brick that made each one stand out in a neat rectangle. In the small front yards there were often decorative plastic figures or small fountains. Pink flamingos in their stereotypical stance—arched neck, one visible leg, hovering over a shallow green plastic pond—were particularly popular and soon became the brunt of jokes among the amused volunteers, only, of course, when no local could hear them. "The flamingos" became volunteer shorthand for the neighborhood in general.

On our side, the Black side, the houses reflected the poverty of the neighborhood, lacking the trim, consciously groomed look seen across the street. But thankfully, the houses were not literally falling apart or boarded up. Our side was rundown but looked lived in, and people did that urban neighborhood thing of sitting on stoops—their outdoor stairs leading from their front door to the sidewalk—and chatting with neighbors or passersby. Sometimes they would sit in windows and do their outdoor chatting that way. In our neighborhood it was not unusual to see and hear a largish dog barking and pawing at the backyard fence that kept one small yard separate from the one next door and the alley beyond. It could be alarming if the fence consisted only of flapping wooden slats and the dog was a Doberman or a German shepherd. The noisy backyard dog seemed the antithesis to the silent front yard flamingo, though both made proud statements about ownership of place.

The whole area—the dense, tightly packed row housing, the narrow cobblestone streets, the great divide between Black and white neighborhoods—all this was new not just to me but to nearly all the volunteers. We had come from places like Massachusetts, California, South Carolina, Ohio, New York, Hawaii, Michigan. Most of us came from homes that were middle class in values if not always, like my own, in family income. Our one Black volunteer was from a small town in South Carolina, more rural than urban. And in keeping with my own history, I found I was the only Asian American volunteer. (Later, I met the man in charge of an organization in our neighborhood that offered after-school programs for adolescent boys and girls. He was originally from India.) I don't think any of us came from a dense, struggling, all-Black neighborhood—from an urban ghetto in the classic sense of the word.

Truthfully, we were all as naive as our appearances indicated. But to be fair, our hearts were in the right place, and we made an enthusiastic dive into the tasks at hand. It's not easy to describe what we did, since much of it was just trying to get to know the people we were now living among, to gain their trust, to listen to what they were thinking, what they wanted and needed to make their neighborhood and their lives easier and more livable. Some of us worked with the staffers who already had up-and-running programs: with preteen girls, with toddlers and preschoolers, with young boys if they could be corralled. The programs were meant to be, at least in part, educational and not only after-school recreation. I worked mostly with the Head Start Program, a job I liked because the children were a pleasure, as hard to resist as most kids that age are, and because the teacher I worked with was knowledgeable, dynamic, energetic, and engaging—all the things one needed to be to work with small, energetic kids and their often wary parents. She was a great on-the-job teacher, and I learned enough from her to acquire the skills, competence, and confidence to continue working with preschoolers after I left St. Martha's.

But the biggest project on the agenda was one that, I think it is fair to say, none of us were prepared for, least of all in the crucial area of skill sets. Several volunteers were working pretty much full-time to renovate an empty row house so we could eventually live there and so that when we left, someone in the neighborhood would get a newly fixed-up home. Since I was working mostly in the preschool, I pitched in to work on the house after school was finished for the day. But no one could deny that not one of us knew the first thing about house renovation. It was the supreme learn-as-you-go project, testing our patience, our egos, our ability to maintain our friendships, and our ability to learn new skills on a daily basis. Somewhere tucked away in one of my boxes of past-life detritus, I have pictures of us hacking away at various tasks—knocking down old walls, painting and plastering new walls, filling large cracks between planks on an uneven floor. I know somewhere in there is a picture of Petey, a young Black man who was there for on-the-job training. He was well-known in the neighborhood as a leader of the young men and teenage boys. In the photo, he holds out a can of paint in one hand while pointing to it with the index finger of his other hand and speaks directly to the camera. He is doing an advertisement for the paint! We were glad to have Petey there to keep us laughing and our mood positive. I think we were supposed to be teaching him our (nonexistent) house-fixing skills, but he ended up teaching us more about the neighborhood and Black lives, especially street life, than we ever taught him. For me, the house project felt too overwhelming to be conquered, and I never quite believed we would get it done. We eventually did finish it, but I can't actually remember living there.

So this was my introduction to Philadelphia and to South Philly in particular. It was not the usual way one moves to a new city to take up residence.

But South Philly was not just a small neighborhood of thriving Italian Americans living across from benighted African Americans enclosed in what everyone was calling "a ghetto." South Philly was a place with a lot of pride in where it was and who was living there—and especially in who had come from there. It didn't take long for us volunteers to learn that the Italian side was the home of Frank Sinatra, and Sinatra references could be seen all over the neighborhood—pictures of a youthful, sweet-faced, blue-eyed rising star on the walls of shops and restaurants, faded LP covers of him in storefront windows, his voice crooning songs he had made famous in the background of many commercial establishments.

On the African American side it was the hit single "Dancin' in the Streets" (which was, in fact, summer recreation for kids of all ages); it was Motown and the Temptations and hits from other Black artists. And it was something else, too, something I would get to learn about, something Black folks had been enjoying as their own for some time. But at that very moment it had begun to get more widely noticed, and some aspects of mainstream culture were promoting it just by being interested in it. It was called jazz.

Black South Philadelphia was physically, geographically, a small area covering only a few square blocks. It was much smaller than its counterpart, North Philadelphia, another mostly African American neighborhood that covered a sizable area and was much better known throughout the region. North Philadelphia received a lot more help from government agencies and other sources for its neighborhood improvement projects. Nevertheless, we in South Philly did have community organizers or social workers of similar ilk, outsiders who were tied to larger social projects—some government-funded—who would periodically visit the "hood" to offer or check on services. It was one such social worker, an African American man who would come by sometimes with his two buddies, who introduced us volunteers to jazz. To be honest, these young but slightly older than us adult men were clearly also coming to see about the VISTA volunteers who had landed in their city and were supposed to be cleaning up poverty here and in cities all over the United States. I'm sure they felt like they'd seen all this before and wanted to check out this new crop of do-gooders.

I think at first these men found our group of earnest volunteers a bit of a curiosity and amusing to watch as we struggled to decipher the street language, a whole new way of using verbs and nouns; to grasp the cultural differences, including my first (and only) experience eating chitlins; to mediate the wariness of some of the residents, tired of feeling like their community was being used for yet another "social experiment." But they were men, and there were more women volunteers than there were men, so their interest brought them back to the neighborhood and St. Martha's on a regular basis. Certainly, they all knew white women just as they knew white men—casually, in public places like supermarkets and schools and in the places where they worked. Maybe they had a few white women friends. But I think they weren't quite sure what to make of me, an Asian American woman, someone clearly not Black but not quite white either. No one, not even the neighborhood residents, ever directly asked me anything about my ethnic background, but sometimes I felt a kind of extra curiosity directed toward me. It was so subtle that I was never sure I was right about it, but sometimes it felt like the glances coming my way lasted a fraction longer than usual or that someone I was talking to had a slightly more quizzical look in their eyes than usual, and often I felt a sincere warmth, a kind of recognition coming from some of the greetings exchanged on the street. Not that the other volunteers experienced any rudeness or hostility or disrespect from any of the neighborhood residents. As I said, I just felt slightly more noticed than the other female volunteers, either in a neutral way or a positive one, never negatively.

So our male visitors—most of them barely older than us—continued to come by and soon most of us, even the guys, came to have conversations with them that were friendly and more personal, relaxed, and fun. In one conversation, one of them asked me what kind of music I liked. I answered, "folk music, you know, guitars and folk singers like Pete Seeger and Joan Baez and Judy Collins." The response I got stopped just short of a condescending scoff. That was not really music, that folk stuff. What about jazz? What did I think about jazz?

My older sister had talked once or twice about jazz; she and her college friends had mentioned names like Stan Kenton, Benny Goodman, Count Basie, Duke Ellington. I had at least heard those names, and, in fact, the latter had performed one night on my college campus. I had gone to hear him and thought his music was okay, but it was not an experience I would need to repeat anytime soon. But my new friend kept pressing me. He insisted that the music we all needed to hear was jazz and that we could hear lots of good jazz right there in Philadelphia. In fact, he could take us to a club some night soon so we would know what he was talking about. And sure enough, that's what happened. Some of us ended up going with him and his friends to hear their music at their favorite club.

The clubs were typically bars with small tables and a little area set apart as a stage—to this day, I consider a jazz club bona fide only if the space is small and the air is swirling with cigarette smoke caught in the shafts of light filtering through the dimly lit room. (Now, of course, given smoking bans, that is not possible in most public places.) In those days, wine was drunk only by "winos" on the street, manhandling a bottle of dark, syrupy sweet Thunderbird or something else equally certain to put you out of commission. The club atmosphere was filled with the clinking of glasses of scotch, vodka, bourbon, gin—the hard stuff—and with muted voices murmuring, punctuated by an occasional raucous laugh. My volunteer friends and I loved it, that grownup, sophisticated feeling, hearing music that much of the general public had yet to catch on to. Music that grabbed our attention and made us listen even as the atmosphere let us kick back and settle into the vibe.

I will be forever grateful to the friends who took us to hear some of the jazz greats in those funky little smoke-filled clubs. Musicians who would later cross over and become famous nationally and even internationally. I remember seeing Miles Davis in a club set up like a theater with just a few rows of theater-like seating. It was a late set, around midnight. Mr. Cool Jazz stepped onto the floor looking slim, trim, and dapper in a suit—the way he always seemed to look in public. He was holding his horn in front of him, and he took a survey of the audience—not a large one at that late hour—moving those large, unblinking eyes of his across the rows of seats, taking in the scene. I guess he wasn't impressed with what he saw because after he'd blown a few perfunctory (but beautiful) bars along with the song playing in the background, he dropped his horn to his side, and very shortly after that he turned his back on us and walked off the floor. That was it. That was all we were going to get. We had been warned about Miles and his style. He wasn't there to make you feel comfortable; he only gave you what he was willing to give you—on his terms. He called the shots. He was Mr. Cool Jazz.

But for me, the real coup d'état was the night a few of us heard John Coltrane play live. He was playing on a small, raised stage with just one other person: his wife, Alice. She was off to the side a little, on the piano. Trane was standing there, front and center, blowing his heart out. He didn't seem concerned about who was in the audience. He was just up there playing. He was bending, twisting, swaying back and forth, his body moving to the music on demand, eyes closed, sweat forming on his hairline and trickling down his face. He was fused to his saxophone, was one with his music. He *was* the music. The notes came soft at first, next to each other. Gliding. Sliding. Then building, one on top of another. Forming layers. Coming up from underneath, slipping in sideways. Growing in density and strength. Struggling, struggling to climb. Climbing. Reaching. Slipping back. Reaching again. And finally, reaching a climax. He let us hang there for an exhilarating moment before once again descending, bringing us gently back to an even line of almost-melody.

I sat with my mouth open, eyes wide, not able to fully grasp the music but enthralled by the intensity, the passion, the truth of the music and the musician. My girlfriend and fellow volunteer sitting next to me, looking equally dazed, turned to me and said, "He just blew an orgasm."

Mostly, I don't talk about my life as a VISTA volunteer. It feels like it is made up of too many strands that can't be gathered up into a nice, neat, symmetrical ball to be bounced casually into cocktail party conversation. But sometimes I take a chance when I'm talking with someone about something that conjures up some vivid aspect of South Philadelphia. If that subject happens to be jazz and the person seems to know about jazz and truly loves and appreciates it, then I might mention my good luck at having heard Coltrane in person. This happened at a party one night not long ago, a party smaller and more intimate than a see-and-be-seen cocktail party. I was talking seriously with a young man, perhaps in his early forties, who had a clear love for the music and knew more about jazz than I did, certainly more than most people of his generation. After an engaging exchange, I told him how lucky I felt to have seen and heard the great John Coltrane. As I described the scene in the club, my young friend listened intently, then asked, "What happened with Alice?"

"Well, she played along for awhile, but it didn't take long before she stopped and just sat quietly at the piano. Eventually, she got up and left the stage. She knew whose moment it was."

We talked a little more about my experience, the musician, and how within a year of my seeing him, Coltrane would be dead. We both were aware that an early death was far too common among the jazz greats of that era.

I could tell that my friend was impressed with my story, so, wanting to lighten the moment, jokingly and with a flourish, I extended my hand, saying, "You may kiss my hand if you like." And to my amusement, he did.

8

Cape Town to Japantown

There are pictures that I never had to cut out and put in the file, ones that are imprinted in my memory.

I had seen the image before, but seeing it at the actual scene of the crime was like seeing it for the first time. The terror of the scene had me paralyzed. I couldn't stop staring at it: a teenage boy runs with the body of a thin, lifeless little boy in his arms. He looks dazed. Not sure where he's going. He's just running. A young girl runs with them, her face contorted in fear. The caption under the picture says that the girl is the dead boy's sister, which makes the scene more horrifying.

I was in South Africa at the Hector Pieterson Museum, standing in front of the iconic picture of Hector. He is memorialized as the first child killed in the Children's Uprising in Soweto in 1976, during the brutal years of apartheid. As I stood on the very spot of earth where the massacre took place, earth soaked with the blood and stories of unarmed children fired upon by well-armed military men, I shuddered from shame. These were children, after all, many dressed in school uniforms. They wanted better schools and they wanted to learn English and they had gathered to tell that to the white government. What could be so scary about them? Yet they were met by soldiers with guns and clubs advancing toward them, some in tanks. I tried to imagine myself at that moment: How would I, a young girl of color, respond in such circumstances? Would I have been at that protest in the first place? Would my parents have let me go? I was pretty sure I'd have had to sneak out and join my friends at a meeting place. Would I have ended up like some of the children—with a bullet in my back as I tried to run away?

It was 2006, a dozen years after apartheid had officially ended, and we were a small group of strangers, academics from various colleges and universities across the United States. My school was in San Francisco where I was a psychotherapist in the student health center. All of us were there to learn about how a country could rise from the bitter ashes of apartheid and build a democratic, inclusive, multicultural government and society. We had been attending fascinating lectures by local professionals describing a vital, colorful South African social and political life, but we had noticed a mysterious silence about the cruel years of apartheid. There was not even a mention of the world-famous Truth and Reconciliation Commission, formed after apartheid was abolished, a particular interest of mine because of my work as a therapist. The commission created the opportunity and the atmosphere for victims of violent crimes and their perpetrators to come together. They faced one another and spoke to each other, eye to eye: one telling what it was like to be an innocent victim of horrendous violence, the other confessing his crime and in some cases asking for forgiveness. This premeditated step toward reconciliation, while not perfect, astonished the world in its boldness and the extent of its success. Other countries have adopted the model to deal with the aftermath of their own violent struggles for freedom and democracy. I wondered, could some form of this model work between two individuals? But the lecturers told us nothing about this soul-wrenching metaphysical struggle or the mighty physical struggle that had taken place to bring their country to its present, triumphant, yet fragile state.

I assumed this muteness on the subject was a result of how unspeakable South Africans considered the topic. What we soon learned was that they had cleverly spared us words to let us have the actual experience, to relive, as best anyone could, moments from that terrifying struggle. They did this by bringing us to several of the most legendary memorial sites in the area and letting us wander. As we trod the ground where men, women, and children had been killed with guns and bombs, banished to prison cells, or evicted from their homes by armed militia and tanks, we could feel the earth around us shake with fear and fury, and it felt as if we were witnessing firsthand a country in the throes of violent turmoil. The past sprang to life, momentarily becoming as real as the present, and momentarily, that present included us.

The Hector Pieterson Museum; the Apartheid Museum outside Johannesburg; Robben Island, where Nelson Mandela was held for eighteen of the twenty-seven years he was imprisoned; the District Six Museum in Cape Town: each of these memorials forced us, me, to stand for at least a few seconds in the shoes of a terrified child or an abused prisoner or a bereft family member. To stand in a person's shoes is to take the person on, to come as close as we can to feeling what they felt in that moment. While I can't presume to have known exactly what that other person felt, my empathy was awakened, and I had many horrifying moments in which I felt I was actually there at the scene; I wasn't just an outsider looking from a far remove.

At the entrance to the Apartheid Museum, the visitor is faced with two entrances, one marked "White," the other "Nonwhite." Though segregation was officially abolished when apartheid was finally dismantled in the early 1990s, this dramatic maneuver immediately introduces the essence of apartheid: one world for whites and a separate one for everyone else—the nonwhite world. I watched my colleagues easily choose one or the other and enter the building. But I stood outside for a long minute trying to sort out which door to use.

Earlier in the trip, one of my colleagues had told me almost off-handedly, "You know, at one time in South Africa's history, the Japanese were considered white." So at that time, I could have entered as "white." As the government became more and more repressive, the "nonwhite" category was expanded to include "Asians," at which point I would have had to enter on the "nonwhite" side. As a child in 1950s Denver, although I stood out from my white friends, I could and did go anywhere with them. This museum entrance was my first experience of having to decide: Was I "white" or "nonwhite?"

But even in South Africa, people were not so easily labeled. One random, stomach-turning test to determine a person's color status was the pencil-in-the-hair test. A pencil was inserted into the hair of the person in question: if it stood up straight, the person was Black; if it fell over, he or she was checked off as "colored," which included a wide range of shades of black and brown, each offering different amenities and restrictions. Given the history of Japanese in the United States and my own experience of duality, I decided to try both entrances to see how each would feel. I first went through the "white" entrance and stood in the entrance hall for awhile. Then I turned around to leave and reenter through the "nonwhite" gate but found I couldn't go back the way I had come in. The revolving entrance gates moved only one way, straight ahead. Instead, I had to stoop under a barrier, and the bending and stooping, gestures of submission, seemed like the perfect metaphor for entering through a "nonwhite" gate. In the end, neither entrance felt right—and how could they, I wondered, feel right for anyone?

Once inside, we witnessed a painful and thorough time machine trip through apartheid. We saw pictures of the major players on both sides of the struggle, including photos of the architects and perpetrators of apartheid: Hendrik Verwoerd, P. W. Botha, Frederik Willem de Klerk. We saw pictures of the murder rained down on the schoolchildren of Soweto at their protest march, though none of the photographs prepared us emotionally for the experience of actually being there later in the week. We watched early newsreels unroll moments of terror—beatings, shootings, night raids on homes—and then encountered the evidence of the work: salvaged objects and broken or damaged household goods and furniture were placed throughout the museum. And we took a sharp inward breath when we recognized pictures of streets and districts and buildings we had already visited and seen firsthand.

Then there were the many images of famous leaders of the ANC, the African National Congress: Walter Sisulu, Oliver Tambo, and, of course, Nelson Mandela. But we noticed that photographs of Mandela in the prime of his middle years did not exist. The apartheid government had early on forbidden any picture or image of him to be shown in public. When he was finally released from prison after twenty-seven tortured years and started to campaign for his presidency, no one was sure what he looked like. All they had to go on was the picture of a husky-looking young boxer facing a sparring partner, gloved fists raised in ready position, and an old poster of a rising lawyer and activist for the ANC, full-faced, determined, his thick hair with a colonial-style part slightly off-center—a line as clear and stark as the separation of the races themselves.

I could wrap my mind around banning a book or a manifesto. But a picture of one person? I finally understood that the fear that drove the brutality of the apartheid regime was absolute, coming from the very top tiers of government, relentlessly soaking the country like waves pounding a pier, the salty water settling into every crack of timber and slowly rotting away the wood. Fear had been rotting away the country until, finally, it had given way. Nelson Mandela won the election in 1994, becoming the first Black president of South Africa. As I exited the museum, my heart gave a quiet cheer that justice, long overdue, had finally arrived.

Robben Island, the prison for the Black African freedom fighters, has been likened to Alcatraz Island, the old prison in San Francisco Bay. Both can be cold, foggy, and windy—spiteful places to be. Both are now only places to visit a not-so-lofty past. Our group escaped the choppy winter boat ride and arrived on Robben Island to sunshine and warmth and still air, which gave the lie to the island's purpose. Despite the many tourists wandering the grounds, the place felt oddly silent, and we, too, were silent as we walked the infamous quarters where Mandela and the freedom fighters had been locked up. Moving somberly along the aisle of cells, our guide, a no-frills kind of man, stopped us and said in a matter-of-fact voice, "This is the cell of prisoner 46664, our most famous prisoner, Nelson Mandela."

Naive perhaps, but I was surprised to see that his cell was like all the rest: tiny, spare, a bucket in the corner for his toilet, and a narrow cot to sleep on. We knew Mandela had a large frame and an even larger spirit. One could sense his size even in pictures in which he was standing alone. Yet his cell was barely large enough for a man to stand with arms extended. My own body fidgeted as I wondered how he kept his sanity, stuffed into that tiny space with so much activity going on in his head. He was, after all, still the leader of the ANC.

In truth, he didn't spend much time there; all the prisoners did hard labor. Stepping outside the cellblock, we moved on to where the prisoners dug up and broke rock all day. The glaring sunlight, magnified by the chalky white limestone, forced us to shade our eyes. The guide was explaining, "Of course, the prisoners were given no protection from the blazing sun, which was made worse by the whiteness of the rock, so Mandela and others suffered permanent damage to their eyes." I was wearing sunglasses and the glare still penetrated my eyes, making me realize another one of those generous acts from Mandela: I'd never seen a picture of him, after his release, wearing protective sunglasses. He knew how much his people, deprived of him and his image for so many years, needed to look into the face and eyes of their charismatic leader to feel optimistic and reassured. Just seeing a picture of him with that signature smile works the same magic for me even now.

Robben Island had once been a home for lepers, and that is how the freedom fighters lived their lives: isolated, cut off from everyone they knew and loved, with the jailers jeering, "You can forget about ever seeing them again. I can promise you that." The landscape here reflected their lives—barren, rocky, lacking any of the smoothed edges brought about by love and tenderness. I left that cruel island wondering how anyone confined there could possibly keep alive the spirit to resist. Despair seemed a much easier route, and I left with a coward's relief that I didn't have to make that choice.

In 1966, bulldozers invaded the area known as District Six in Cape Town. The noise was deafening as they rumbled in and smashed homes and stores and business buildings to pieces. At the time, this desirable area of Cape Town was a "colored" neighborhood, a mix of "nonwhite" ethnic groups and religions. "Blacks" had been banned long before. Former residents will tell you that it was run-down, that the buildings and streets needed repair, and that the public services were sub-par. Still, it was home to around 60,000 people; it was their community and they had friends, businesses, schools, churches, synagogues, and mosques to call their own. Even if it looked worn out, it was thriving, vital, and mostly stable. People went to work and school and returned home in the evening. Families and children knew each other; people gossiped on street corners and interacted in public without conflict over their religious or ethnic differences. But the apartheid government had long been eying District Six and wanted it for a "whites-only" district.

So in 1966 the government forces made their move, scattering the community and sending the residents to the outskirts of town, to the undesirable "barren Cape Flats." There the congenial mix of residents was separated, parsed according to their official ethnic groups: "Cape Coloreds, Cape Malays, Indians"—a standard apartheid strategy to break down resistance.

The residents of District Six tried to hold on to their neighborhood, but they were no match against the full might of the government. They lost their struggle, but they were determined not to be smashed and destroyed like so much timber and concrete, not to be buried so they disappeared completely, not to be treated as if none of them had ever existed. In their determination to hold on to themselves and to each other, they came up with an ingenious idea: they would create a memorial, not just to their former homes and lives but a space that would honor and recognize all South Africans who had been forcefully removed from their homes. These displaced souls would have a place to visit to feel remembered and understood, to recharge their hope. A project full of heart and compassion. The result was the District Six Museum. It opened its doors in 1994.

To step into the museum is to feel like you are out for a walk and have happened onto this inviting old neighborhood. Everything about it gave me a feel for the streets and homes and the people who lived there. What caught my attention at once were some slightly battered but original street signs hanging ladder-like from the ceiling: Hanover, Constitution, Vernon Terrace, and others less grand. These signs had been hidden away during the initial bulldozing, then remembered later by a former resident, dug up, and cleaned. Now they were hanging here, giving a new sense of direction. On the floor in front of the ladder of signs was a large map of the old neighborhood, showing streets and landscapes. It is lovingly signed by some of the former residents on the very spots where they used to live. Running my fingers over the names and gentle undulations of the streets, I could feel through my fingertips some of the old neighborhood pride. Then I meandered on, walking through the display of long, brightly colored banners hanging next to each other from the ceiling. Each was adorned with the symbol of one of the four major religious groups represented in District Six: Islam, Judaism, Christianity, and Hinduism. The twisted irony of replacing this neighborhood of ethnic and religious harmony with the monolithic, monochromatic imperative of apartheid brought a cynical smile to the corners of my mouth.

I was ambling along, taking in the sights, listening for sounds of the old neighborhood—balls bouncing on sidewalks, friends calling out greetings—when I happened upon a complete little room fully restored to look exactly as it had before its occupants (two sisters, Thelma and Nuvuyo) were forced out. My feet stopped, refusing to move on. Something was telling me that I'd been here before. How could that be, I wondered? Intrigued, I stepped in. I found a clean, basic room, modestly furnished with signs of everyday life: curtains on windows, a plain bed covered with a patterned quilt, a simple wood table, a cooking pot blackened from years of use, family photos on the walls. Everything just as it had been when the family members left for the day to go to work or school. The little room felt loved and comfortable, filled with sweetness. There was something else, too. But before I could figure out what that something else was, I found myself—as though suddenly transported through a Star Trek wormhole, a shortcut through space-time—in a different room in a different museum, one in San Francisco.

That other room was a family's "home," a barracks room in a World War II incarceration camp for Japanese Americans. Executive Order 9066 had been implemented quickly, given the usually torpid government bureaucracy, sending all the incarcerees—two young generations of American-born citizens and the first generation, their elderly immigrant parents and grandparents—off to crude, rapidly constructed, military-style barracks: long buildings divided into "apartments" usually consisting of only one large room. These structures were not adequate as "homes" and only slightly better than the horse stables some had been moved to initially while waiting for the barracks to be completed. The barracks were thrown up in ten locations around the country, expressly chosen for their scorching, sandy deserts or hot, humid swamplands or cold, snowy mountains and plains. The shoddy construction left wide cracks between the wall planks that let in everything—heat, cold, wind, snow, sand, and rain. The residents still had to enter through a door.

At that San Francisco museum so many years before, I had stepped inside a reconstructed barracks room meant for an entire family. My heart dropped as I took in the sight: nothing more than a makeshift cabin good only for temporary escape from a storm. One could not even call such a home modest. The beds were government-issue army cots; the residents had cleverly constructed crude-looking tables and chairs from odds and ends found around the camp. At first, I was puzzled by a line strung from one wall to the opposing wall, with a blanket thrown over it. When I realized this was supposed to create a separate "room," I felt mortified for the young couples, the largest group of incarcerees. When they wanted a moment of intimacy, did they simply throw modesty aside? Knowing Japanese propriety, my imagination hit a roadblock. A dim light glared from a single bare bulb hung from another line stretched across the ceiling. How did parents dedicated to education get their children to read or study at night when they could barely see? Family pictures on the walls seemed a wan attempt to add decoration and warmth to the space, and they served the additional purpose of reminding the residents of the loved ones they had been separated from, sometimes not knowing where they had been taken.

In Cape Town, in Thelma and Nuvuyo's room, the images of the barracks room in San Francisco swirled around me. I was mesmerized, caught in the thrall of this completely familiar experience halfway around the world from my home. And then it came to me, what that "something else" was that I was feeling along with the warmth and love that permeated this space: it was sorrow. The sorrow was palpable and clung to me like cloth. The same was true for the barracks room in San Francisco. In one room, sorrow for what was at the present; in the other, sorrow for what no longer was.

I no longer puzzled over why I had felt from the moment I entered the District Six Museum that I knew this place, that I had been here before, that I had already witnessed this dislocation. It was history, my history, tugging at me for attention. There it was again, the forced removal. My parents and sister, forced out of their modest but comfortable Seattle apartment, where my father was going to the University of Washington at night and working by day and my mother was raising her little girl in the community of other young Japanese American mothers. Suddenly, by government decree, they had to leave all that behind. The story I knew so well, returning where I'd least expected it.

I could hear my mother, distraught, trying to pack: "Oh no, we can't leave that, we might need it. And that was a wedding gift. What will we say when Ray and Ethel come to visit and they don't see it on display?" And my father, gently trying to break through her denial, which is more like disbelief ("It wasn't supposed to be this way"): "Now wait a minute. We can't take that. We don't have room, wedding gift or not. You know what they said—only what we can carry. That's it. That's all we can take."

So they packed up the few material possessions they could carry in their suitcases and, trying not to look back, took off for my father's parents' small farm in Wyoming, outside the zone in which their presence was considered a "security risk." Had it not been for this arbitrary circumstance, my family would also have ended up in a camp, and on my birth certificate would be the made-up name of a humiliating incarceration camp rather than the town of Sheridan. My first room might have looked like this one, as bare and makeshift and full of both love and sorrow.

The barracks room exhibit was the center of a larger display of San Francisco's Japantown, or J-Town as the locals called it. I left the barracks and in a few short steps stood under the street signs at the corner of Post and Laguna. Even after the war, this corner remained in the heart of J-Town. As an adult in San Francisco and later in the East Bay, when I would start to run low on supplies, I would make an excursion there to shop at my favorite markets for all the Japanese foods I couldn't get at Safeway or the Berkeley Co-op. Then, with supplies in tow, I would have udon for lunch at my favorite restaurant, make a stop at the sweet shop in the corner of the mall for my manju fix, and finally head back across the bay for home.

In the District Six Museum, I left Thelma and Nuvuyo's room, and my feet took me back to the ladder of street signs, the heart of the museum display. I was surprised when I noticed where I was standing, as I didn't remember walking there. I shook my head to come back to the present and made a feeble attempt to continue my tour of the museum. But like a sleepwalker, I moved around but wasn't really awake. Finally, I gave up and left the building. Outside on the sidewalk, I looked up at the sky, blue and lightly clouded through filtered winter sunlight, and drank in a deep breath of fresh air.

I wasn't born when my parents and sister were forced to leave Seattle, but their eviction and relocation has lived in me as well, creating a legacy for me to reckon with. My parents, my family, may have mercifully escaped going to an incarceration camp, but they also missed the opportunity to share their plight with anyone who was at all like them—in appearance or experience. They were thrust into a hostile white world and made to maneuver a safe path through it, for themselves but, more important, for their children. They were isolated. Surely they were feeling anger, fear, confusion, and despair; but there was nothing to be done about it, no one to talk to, so it was best not to speak of it at all, just put it behind them and move on. Survival was the goal.

In South Africa, the brilliance and power of the memorials and museums we witnessed lay in their capacity to inform as well as to make the viewer remember. They announce to the world what happened. They make the events public. Some viewers remember; some become aware for the first time. But what happened is not forgotten. The memory of all that happened lives on in the open air; it does not remain embedded in the soul to be silently passed on to future generations, to remain buried in their hearts, to deceive them into thinking it is something they have done that has brought about their suffering and that now they are on their own with nowhere to turn, no one to help them. And most damning of all—to keep them quiet.

Seeing a piece of my personal history played out in Cape Town, half a world away from my home, was both shocking and comforting. The experience remains close to my heart, as does that image of Hector Pieterson. It made me realize that human cruelty and brutality are the same no matter where they happen—they can even take the same shape. But I was also reassured that we know what to do to fight against the evil we have done to one another: no matter where we are, we must cast light on the truth, and we must remember.

9

Chicken, Waffles, and . . . Tsukemono

One thing you won't find in my "permanent" file is a single recipe. I don't like to cook. I do like to eat.

This is not a good combination unless you get lucky and end up living with a chef or with someone who is interested in all aspects of food or with someone who really likes to cook not only for the pleasure it brings her or him but also for the praise from friends who rave about the meal afterward. Or unless, like me, you live in a place that makes a near religion out of food—growing it, cooking it, and serving it in restaurants ranging from expensive and high end to modest and affordable. All with better-than-average fare.

As an adult, I got lucky. I happen to live only a couple of miles from North Berkeley, home of the famed "gourmet ghetto." So when I am feeling lazy or sick of my own cooking or both, I can either go out to eat or get tasty, freshly made takeout to bring home. A big plus to eating in Berkeley is that you can get practically any kind of food you want, from local and fancy California cuisine to the range of Asian cuisines—not just the standard Chinese and Japanese fare but also Korean, Cambodian, Vietnamese, Malaysian, Burmese . . . And the Chinese is broken down into Hunan, Szechuan, Taiwanese; spicy to mild; or perhaps just Northern and Southern. Then there is a plethora of Italian restaurants, some also advertising themselves as from specific areas like Naples, Venice, or Milan; a few Greek cafés and coffee shops; and a number of Indian places, also differentiating themselves by Northern or Southern, spicy to mild. This being California, there are numerous Mexican eateries, ranging from the everyday taco to dishes rarely found outside of Mexico. We have one seriously famous French-style café and restaurant that has taken both California and French cuisine to new, creative levels, and there are a few other French bistros within city limits. I've even noticed one or two Afghan restaurants. I know of a single British pub, a holdout, but the few remaining Irish pubs I can think of are in San Francisco. In the past I noticed a German place or two, but I'm not sure they still exist. There are a few plain old burger joints with more than decent burgers and fries; Berkeley is, after all, a college town. Oh, and how about that little Eritrean place on Telegraph Avenue that I have yet to check out . . .

I must confess, all this great food is one of the things that keeps me tied to Berkeley. That and the weather and the intellectual stimulation and the diverse population—people of all skin tones and physical features, speaking all kinds of languages, some of which I cannot identify just from hearing them on the street. So that's a lot of reasons for staying in Berkeley and the Bay area.

Food looms large in explaining why we Berkeley-ites so enjoy our city's above-average human diversity. The food itself is just a welcome by-product of the fact that the people who make it have come from all those places and now live here in Berkeley. The owners and managers of the cafés and restaurants have found a way to make a living by capitalizing on their culture and sharing it in a most intimate manner. This famous aspect of small-town Berkeley, this exceptional eating opportunity, has brought tremendous pleasure to the majority of people who live here and certainly to me. Partly because, as I have confessed, I hate to cook.

I don't have an explanation for why this is. I've always assumed that people, men and women, were born either liking to cook or not. I have a great-nephew, all of eleven years old, who loves to cook and who even when he was much younger enjoyed stirring up a bowl of flour and water his mother let him play with. I happen to fall into the latter category.

When I was growing up, some version of meat and potatoes—at our house, that was meat and rice—with a few seasonal vegetables thrown in was pretty much standard farm fare for lunch and dinner. In fact, for farm families, "dinner" was our noon meal, and "supper" was what we ate in the evening. "Lunch" was what we kids took to school in our lunchboxes.

Unlike a city kid, I never once thought that milk came from cartons; I had firsthand experience with where it came from, and that was true of other foods as well. I took for granted the fact that we always had fresh eggs since I frequently was the one who had to gather them from the chicken coop, sometimes stealing them right out from under the hen so I didn't have to go back a second time that day. As I child, I never questioned the fact that during the growing season we had fresh vegetables. Mom always had a small garden, and my grandparents grew vegetables for a living. I also took for granted that we usually had meat available because on occasion Dad might slaughter a pig or a cow, and someone else in the area had often slaughtered one of their animals and was selling the lamb or beef or pork.

If you know geography or look on a map, you can see that Montana's northern boundary borders on Canada. Our little town of Hardin was closer to the southeast border of the state, around 250 miles from the Canadian border. That still puts it pretty far north, and that means living in well-defined seasons—living with the weather. Summers in Hardin could get "burning" hot, and winters were certainly freezing cold. Spring was the welcome reminder—there was nothing trite about it—that after a long winter, life can and does renew itself. And fall felt so pleasant, with the cottonwoods turning gold and the tangy air relieving us from the heat, merely hinting at the harsh winters that lay ahead. As the seasons changed, we changed our clothing to keep pace with the weather. In Hardin, everyone had a true summer wardrobe and a completely different one for winter. Going from the intense heat of summer to the extreme cold of winter, we kids would go from wearing as little as we could get away with to gradually adding layer after layer until finally we were bundled up in heavy jackets, mittens, mufflers, hats, and skid-proof boots.

I can remember walking to Grandma's house in the summer heat, and while the actual distance from our house to hers was short, probably less than a mile, it felt like miles. Usually, I was with my sisters, and we would plod along the gravel road, moving in slow motion but wanting to get to her house fast so we could get inside and cool off. Cooling off was just getting out of the sun. No one I can remember had air conditioning, at least not when we were kids. So inside Grandma's house, the air was still overheated, but after our walk, it was a relief. Every household had a fan or several fans—big square ones, little round ones—positioned strategically around the house, and Grandma had them, too. They did move the air around—some—and help cool it down.

In the winter, it was the opposite. We would walk the distance as fast as our legs would carry us, all the while puffing out breaths of warm air that would materialize as soon as they hit the cold air. Once at Grandma's door, we would kick off our boots and race inside to the living room heater where we could unthaw.

I wasn't on the farm long enough to really understand much about growing crops—which ones needed a lot of summer heat, which ones needed lots of water, which ones less water, which ones to plant when. And frankly, as a kid, I could have cared less. The farmers in the valley had figured out what crops were suited to the extreme Montana weather. Because of how far north we were, I presume the growing season was shorter than in some of the other Plains states, and that meant the season for gathering fresh food directly from the garden was short. The farmers' wives did what they could to raise gardens of plenty, both to give their families fresh veggies during the summer and to have enough to can for the winter months. The word *canning* is a misnomer since cans were never used. It was always jars, mostly Mason jars with the name on the jar, the letters molded into the glass. I have vague memories of Grandma and Mom canning fruit but not vegetables. And I have fond and delicious memories of eating Grandma's canned cherries, which were so red and plump and sweet, it seemed like she had opened a jar of rare elixir whenever she served us any. The juice was so red, a deep wine-red, that it would stain whatever it touched. She also had excellent canned peaches, and while cherries and peaches were not home-grown fruits, large quantities of them must have been brought to the stores in town during their peak season for her to get enough to can. My ignorance of these details is another example of my liking to eat and not caring how the finished product got to my plate or palate.

Women had been filling pressure cookers to can Mason jars full of produce for many long years, but in our valley, the game-changer for preserving food was the home freezer. I remember my parents suddenly talking about this brand-new home appliance that some farm wives were buying for their kitchens or back porches. It was called just that—a freezer—and was shaped like an oversized chest with a pull-up / fold-down lid, like the ones that today we call coolers and take on our long road trips or camping trips. While these coolers are small, made to be stuffed in the backseat or trunk of the car, the new home freezer was huge, more like a refrigerator turned on its side. The farmer's wife would need a spot large enough to position such a hefty new contraption. And I imagine the price tag for something still fairly unusual was pretty hefty as well. Given these variables, not everyone could buy one right off, but the idea, the possibility, of freezing your produce instead of canning it took off like wildfire. Housewives all over the valley started freezing their vegetables. The idea was to clean and parboil the beans or peas or whatever, pack them into cellophane bags, seal them, and then pack the bag into a slick-feeling box, most likely wax-coated to hold up better in the cold. Then label and date the box, and voila! Ready for the freezer. I remember at least one season and possibly more when several of the wives in the valley, friends of Mom's and Grandma's, assembled at Grandma's to freeze veggies, with my sisters and me standing by at the ready. That day we were doing green beans. We formed an assembly line: one woman to wash them, snip off the ends, and cut each bean into the right length; a couple of other women to blanch them and then rinse them in cold water for the next woman, who would pack them in the cellophane bags; the last woman to seal the bag, put it into a box, and label it. My guess is that the community effort was as much about supporting each other in mastering this new freezing technology as it was about getting the job done.

The excitement was pretty high when Mom opened the first box of frozen beans to have for dinner one night early that winter. They looked good, still a nice, fresh, bright-green color; even when they were cooked, they didn't look dull and brown as canned beans tended to. But what a disappointment to the taste. Nothing at all like a fresh green bean. They had what I could only call "the frozen food taste." It was hard to describe but the food, regardless of what it was, was typically imbued with this strange, unnatural, mechanical taste that made every vegetable taste pretty much like every other vegetable. Something had definitely been done to it. Our table at dinnertime was normally not very noisy. We were not a talkative family to begin with, and when it came to random chatter, I was usually the one everyone else pointed to. But I don't remember saying much that night about the beans. I think it was Mom who finally made some comment about how they didn't quite measure up to expectations, and then the subject was dropped—for good.

But the process wasn't dropped. Mom, along with the rest of the housewives, continued to freeze vegetables, probably in the hope that something would improve along the way and the food would start to taste more like the vegetables from their gardens. There was also a widespread belief, possibly floated by the freezer manufacturers, that frozen food was better for you than canned food, more nutritious because it had not been exposed to long minutes of high heat that destroyed nutrients. This helped keep housewives in the game, experimenting on just about every vegetable in the garden to see how it would turn out. Corn was frozen both on and off the cob. Freezing corn off the cob meant adding the step of shearing the kernels off the cob with a sharp knife. This took practice, and some women became adept at cutting off large swaths of kernels in a single stroke, moving up and down the cob held upright in the opposite hand. The piles of kernels were then bagged, boxed, and frozen. Corn, green beans, and peas survived best, but none of them tasted like much. Maybe the best way to describe frozen food in those experimental days is that it was tasteless except for that "frozen food taste" that had little to do with the vegetable's original flavor. Despite the effort it took to freeze vegetables, I think it was still easier than canning, which is probably why freezing became so popular among housewives.

Farmers are hearty eaters; they need healthy food and lots of it to do their work, and meat was high on that list. Even on our small farm, we slaughtered a few animals whenever we could manage to spare one. Of course, we killed chickens to eat immediately, as well as to freeze for future use. There wasn't a farm that didn't have a few chickens pecking and strutting around the yard, both for fresh eggs and for the occasional fried or roasted bird. Some younger chickens were designated as "fryers," while the older, tougher ones were left for their eggs and for breeding. It is also true that if you don't hold on to the chicken after cutting its head off, it will run around headless, spattering blood wherever it goes. A gruesome, if not puzzling, sight. It didn't seem unusual to see Mom dismember a chicken, plucked clean, for dinner. But it was a little disquieting to see the carcass of a calf hanging from a crossbar, its body split open, drained of its blood, waiting to be cut into the sections we see in supermarkets labeled as roasts or steaks or whatever cut the shopper might fancy. I don't remember seeing this often, but I do carry images of it in my memory. Not only of a calf but also of pigs. On our farm, slaughtering for food never took place on a large scale. We just wanted to get through the winter.

My family never owned a separate chest-style freezer. As in most refrigerators today, our fridge on the farm had a separate but small freezer compartment. It certainly wasn't big enough to hold all the boxes of vegetables Mom prepared with the other housewives, and after we had freshly slaughtered pork and beef to add to the supply, such a freezer compartment would have been grossly inadequate. To remedy this problem, Mom and Dad, like many other farmers in the valley, rented space in the big commercial freezer in town. This freezer was a big room kept cold enough so that everything inside would stay frozen until taken out. The room was located behind a narrow, average-looking office that customers would enter first before going to the freezer room in back. Every customer must have had her own section with a number to help locate her food, since Mom always knew exactly where to go to find ours. Sometimes I would go to the freezer with her to pick up some of our meat. To get inside, we would pass through the office and then have to push open the door that looked way too big and heavy for Mom to handle, though she somehow always managed it with ease. We would walk through and be hit immediately with an invisible wall of freezing cold air, which Mom stepped through without hesitating, pulling me along. Then she would stop for a moment to adjust to the blast and to get her bearings so she could go directly to our section of the room and retrieve what she wanted. The room looked like a big storeroom with wide aisles between lots of shelves reaching high up, every shelf filled with packages of all sizes. I remember the floor and walls being concrete, which gave it an even colder feeling.

Every time we went, I was terrified that we would get stuck inside and freeze to death. Mom would forget how to operate the big door or would suddenly be unable to manage its size—or worse yet, she would get lost among the rows of shelves that all looked the same and wouldn't be able to get us out of there. I would run through a quick scenario in my head: I could yell and scream, but I had little confidence that we would be heard from inside this frozen fortress; I could pound on walls or grab things from the shelves and throw them against the door. But I was pretty sure no one would find us in time and when they did, we would be as stiff as statues, as frozen as the meat we had come to pick up. We would just have to hope that someone else would come in to pick up their goods before we froze to death. What scared me the most was that huge door. I never quite trusted that it could be moved—especially by my petite mother.

I never mentioned my fears to Mom, I never created a scene or refused to go in with her and help her carry things out, and my fears never materialized. We always came and went, likely within a matter of minutes. I don't remember when we stopped using that freezer in town, but it was probably when Grandma got a freezer chest and shared it with us. She never knew how much terror she kept me from reliving.

Before freezing and even before canning, there was tsukemono, a food we grew up with and ate on a regular basis. The polite definition for tsukemono is "fermented vegetables," all manner of fermented vegetables.

I say that fermented is the polite word because I have heard tsukemono described as "spoiled or rotten vegetables." I find this a little harsh and not exactly accurate. Today, especially here in California, the concept of fermented food is in no way foreign or unusual, and it would never be thought of as spoiled or rotten. In fact, certain fermented foods have caught on and are popular, even hip, in almost every foodie circle. Non-Asian people as well as Asians can be seen in Asian markets or the Asian section of supermarkets buying jars of tsukemono or of kimchi, its very popular Korean counterpart. Most of these folks think no more of eating these foods than they would of eating sauerkraut. Like sauerkraut and kimchi, tsukemono are vegetables that have been purposely left to sit in brine, with perhaps some vinegar added—the best culinary description for them might be "pickled." The end product is salty, as to be expected, and usually crunchy, though they can also be soft or even wilted depending on the type of vegetable. Sometimes they even taste sweet.

For people who do not consider themselves foodies or have not grown up with tsukemono, their contact with these pickles would most likely occur at a Japanese restaurant where the little side dishes accompanying the main dish are small tastes of different tsukemono. They often come in different colors and shapes—round circles of neon yellow, short stalks of purple, and whitish, light-green shreds. (That would be the typical serving: *takuan*, a round white daikon dyed bright yellow; deep-purple eggplant; and shredded cabbage.) Perhaps this combination of textures, colors, and flavors is what makes the food so popular, but it is also probably the fact that in the years before refrigeration, making tsukemono was a practical way of preserving fragile foods like fresh vegetables and keeping them all year long. Granted, usually the original plant could barely be recognized in the tsukemono served in a restaurant.

Mom never got into making tsukemono, but Grandma continued to make at least a few kinds for as long as she lived on her farm. I think Mom resisted for good reason: she never wanted to appear as if she were competing with Grandma in any way. In truth, she would have been no match for Grandma, since Grandma had the technique down pat. She'd been doing this all her life; she had her special bowls, vats, plates, and the best rocks; and she enjoyed doing it. She especially liked the positive response she received from everyone who tasted the end result. Mom, in contrast, never really learned how anyone made tsukemono, and she had spent so much time living the city life in Seattle that this kind of country cooking eluded her. I don't think she minded leaving this particular task to Grandma. Everyone knew Grandma was a good cook, and tsukemono were just another of her popular dishes.

As a callow youth, I never learned the details of how Grandma made her tsukemono. What I do remember is being in her root cellar, a dank underground storage space hollowed out of the ground and retaining its earthen walls and floor. But Grandma, being resourceful and interested in modern conveniences, had electricity in her storage dungeon, and the walls were lined with shelves. It was clean, orderly, and light; and it had only a slight smell of fresh earth, which was not at all offensive and made it smell like the outdoors. This was the place where foods, especially root vegetables, were kept to preserve as long as possible and also where the jars of canned food were stored. On the floor, out of the way, was a large bowl or vat covered with a plate with a hefty rock on top of it. Underneath the plate, soaking in a salty brine, was a vegetable being turned into tsukemono. It could have been cabbage (napa or regular) or eggplant (Japanese or regular) or long daikon cut into shorter sections. Those were the usual suspects undergoing their transformation, throwing off the not so mild or pleasant smell of fermenting organic plant life. Grandma kept an eye on the vat, and when she determined that the contents were ready, she would transfer them to a bowl and bring it into the light and into the house. Whatever it happened to be got a thorough rinse, was cut into small pieces, and was served along with dinner—steamed rice and usually Japanese-style stir-fry.

I do not think this description does justice to the result, the actual taste of the tsukemono. We kids grew up liking it without question. It was salty, tangy, or maybe sweet and sour combined; it retained a mild flavor of the original vegetable; and, above all, it was crunchy. Something about crunch goes a long way with kids. And the smelly fermentation process never affected the taste in a negative way. It seemed to disappear with the rinse water. That is, until we moved to the city.

After we moved to the city, Mom had to go to the Japanese market and buy all our Japanese food including tsukemono, which came in jars or little cans. But trapping the pickled veggies in jars or cans also trapped the fumes, and to open a jar of white daikon that had turned yellow in the pickling process was to unleash the original odor of vegetable fermentation in full strength. If the Richter scale could measure odor, those jars of *takuan* would have been a solid seven or maybe an eight. In the city, there was no place for the smell to go but into the far reaches of any room to which the air would carry it. Usually, it didn't matter; it was just our family sitting around the dinner table. But when my brother got older and started to bring his mostly white friends home or they would drop by our house at off hours of the afternoon or evening, he put his foot down.

Mom, hand in a half turn on the lid of a jar of *takuan* tsukemono, got the order: "Mom! Stop! Don't open that jar! Ricky [or Tom, Dick, or Harry] is coming by later tonight, and I don't want that stuff smelling up the house." Mom, with a half turn of the lid in the other direction, obeyed the order. I was on my own by then, living away from home, so while I didn't witness any of this firsthand, I learned about it from my sisters and from Mom. They would recount George's behavior in mock horror at his bossy demands, but underneath, I could tell they were amused.

What never got discussed was that banning tsukemono from the dinner table was a graphic example of the fact that in the city, we were pretty much alone as Japanese in our neighborhood and our schools. Tsukemono were another example of our bifurcated existence and how we had to keep our two worlds separate but each fairly intact.

Back on the farm, the few times a year when the Japanese American farm community would get together for fun and relaxation, food always played a central role. The Fourth of July picnics were prime examples of these infrequent gatherings. There would be tables piled with food. There were always standard American-style picnic dishes like potato salad, green salad, baked beans, sometimes corn on the cob, and a dish or two of whatever other vegetables might be in season. There would also be Japanese dishes, especially plain white rice and sushi—the *inari* in their tan burlap-like bags and the circles of *maki*, rolled rice filled in the center with cut veggies and a little fish, surrounded with black seaweed—some teriyaki chicken, and a container or two of someone's tsukemono. The barbeque would be fired up for hotdogs and hamburgers.

When it was time for the main event, time to eat, everyone would take a paper plate with chopsticks for the grownups and plastic forks for the kids and walk along the tables picking up the food they wanted, filling their plates as if seconds didn't exist. Everyone seemed to know which wife had brought which dish, and comments could be heard: "Oh good, Kay made her teriyaki chicken again" or "looks like this is Lois's potato salad" or "here's Ethel's maki sushi, so neat, neh" or "Shirley makes baked beans taste so fancy!" In Japanese style, the cook was not singled out and praised to her face, but people knew and they made their pleasure known in general, and the housewife got the message.

Our Grandma Saito, my father's mother, was an excellent cook and had a bit of a reputation in the area. Not that anyone singled her out either, but folks knew that when they ate her cooking, they would not be disappointed. Without a doubt, they would be eating tasty, well-prepared food. What was atypical for a woman of her generation was that Grandma Saito not only made tsukemono and other Japanese foods exceptionally well, she also baked bread, made handmade ramen noodles, and cooked waffles that could almost float off your plate. It was another way she was ahead of her time in bridging the East-West cultural divide, though that was not her conscious intention.

With the bread, I can only remember the aroma, that unmistakable, mouthwatering smell of bread right out of the oven. We must have still been living in Wyoming during that time, since I don't have memories of her making her own bread when we lived in Hardin. But I do remember the way it smelled and the way it tasted covered with fresh homemade butter and homemade berry jam. The top crust was slightly crunchy, and the bread itself was soft and porous compared to store-bought loafs, so it was easy to go through a lot of bread at a single sitting. Eating fresh-from-the-oven bread puts one forever on a quest to find a bakery that can replicate that taste, but alas, not even in Berkeley's gourmet ghetto have I found such a bakery.

Grandma's waffles were also hard to replicate; they were so light and fluffy and unlike the typical, decent waffles one could get anywhere else. Sitting around her table, we kids would watch patiently but with mounting anticipation as Grandma waited for the waffle iron to heat to the right temperature—I seem to remember a tiny red dot of a light that would go off when the iron was ready—and then she would lift the lid and fill the waffled space with her batter, making sure to cover each section evenly. I can clearly picture her family-sized waffle iron with four oblong sections, good for feeding a big crew of hungry kids who weren't keen on taking turns to get their own hot waffle. When the waffle was ready and the light again went out, four hungry kids each got their own section of fluffy hot waffle, which we immediately smothered in fresh-churned butter and syrup. Grandma was thinking ahead when she bought that four-section machine.

We didn't have a waffle iron at our house, but I remember watching our mother make pancakes, looking on as she filled her blue mixing bowl with flour, eggs, butter, and milk, then beat the batter—not too much or it would go flat and the pancakes wouldn't rise, not enough and the dough would be lumpy. To my mind, flat would have been better than lumpy, since what could be worse than a bite full of flour and a little raw egg. Mom would put a dollop of batter on the steaming hot griddle, and I would give it a few seconds to see how she did. It was always a little magical to watch the raw flat dough start to rise, growing higher, forming little bubbles around the edges of the rising pancake until the edges looked brown and crispy. Then Mom would nudge her spatula under it and—flip! The brown side was up and the raw topside was now down and browning away. Mom got to be an expert at watching the cakes rise just enough and then flipping them over with a deft flick of her wrist. After I left home and was on my own, I would occasionally get an intense craving for homemade pancakes. Having vivid memories of watching Mom make pancakes, I decided to try for myself. I had watched often enough and knew what to look for, so how hard could it be? What I found is that it takes a bit of practice to flip a pancake and end up with an actual round one instead of one that was only part round and had one straight side or one that had broken in two on its way back down to the grill or one that looked more oblong or square and not at all like the circle it had started out as. I had to eat many of my distorted pancakes before I could serve a nearly perfect round one.

I knew that Grandma's waffles tasted different from Mom's pancakes—the waffles were somehow lighter, more weightless. I never knew why until one day I watched Grandma making her batter. Now I know the trick to peerlessly light waffles, a trick not every cook may be aware of, a trick not mentioned on the box of store-bought batter. Just before putting the batter onto the hot waffle iron, Grandma folded in a separate mixture of egg whites beaten into a stiff meringue. No wonder they nearly melted in your mouth. It's a pity that this tidbit of fine cooking was lost on me, the non-cook. I do own a waffle iron, and I have served waffles on a few special occasions when fresh berries are in high season and I want to impress visitors from out of state. The point then is the fresh, succulent berry mélange. The waffles, needless to say, are made from a store-bought batter mix, sans the need for beaten egg whites.

Although her waffles and bread were worth mentioning, Grandma's tour de force was her homemade noodles. She could have made noodles for any dish she wanted, but she always stuck to making them for traditional bowls of steaming hot ramen. Making her own ramen noodles was a labor-intensive job, so when she decided to make them for us, she would marshal her forces—that is, us kids—to help her. Perhaps the only time she could manage to make noodles was when we were around to give her a hand. At any rate, the important item that made it at all possible was the noodle machine, a hand-cranked metal contraption that was screwed to the edge of a table or counter and, when fed a slice of dough, would send strands of fine noodles out the other end. That was the last step, the actual appearance of long strands of noodles that had to be laid out lengthwise on sheets of butcher paper dusted with flour or perhaps cornstarch to keep them from sticking back together. Before that, there was the making of the dough, which Grandma would knead to her own specifications of firmness. She would then roll it out on the table and cut it into sections around six inches wide, which would fit the width of the noodle machine. One of us kids would feed the dough into the machine, another of us would crank the handle, and whoever was left would help Grandma take the strands of noodles exiting from the other end and get them onto the sheets of dusted paper.

We thought it was great fun. I am now betting that Grandma thought it was a pain in the neck but something she was willing to do just to make us happy.

What was mysterious to Grandma was that after the labor-intensive, time-consuming nuisance of hand-making her noodles, making a clear broth to go over them, and serving them fresh and piping hot in the appropriate noodle bowls, none of us kids could ever manage to eat more than a single bowl—albeit a single large bowl. She may have felt that we were disappointed in the noodles, or she may have been remembering what it was like to serve her noodles to hungry working farmers, or maybe she served them in one of the restaurants earlier in her life. Whatever her motivation, she always wanted us to eat more, but we were small kids loving the food, doing the best we could, but only making a dent in the piles of noodles we'd made earlier that day. The noodles were heavy, not thick like fettuccini but fatter and denser than the Italian spaghetti we have become familiar with. A single bowl of Grandma's noodles went a long way.

• • •

Nowhere more than on a farm can one see the symbiosis of work and survival because most of the work has something to do with food, all the steps from growing to processing to preserving it. Many farm kids were members of their local 4-H clubs, which offered programs and projects that gave them an early start in navigating these various steps. Throughout the valley where I grew up, parents loved 4-H because kids of nearly any age could find a relevant project to do through their local chapter.

I don't remember how all three of us sisters got involved in 4-H. It was probably because our parents thought it would be good for us to have some after-school activities. Like most 4-H clubs, ours sponsored and supported crop and animal projects as well as home economics projects like sewing and canning—all the kinds of things farmers and farmers' wives had been doing for decades. It was pretty much taken for granted that the finished products would be entered into the county or state fair competitions, where they would be judged and awarded ribbons. When I moved to California after graduating from college, I was surprised to learn that 4-H clubs play an important role in the fairs that still take place in California farm country.

We sisters did the standard girl tasks like canning fruit, making jam, and sewing skirts and blouses, all under our mother's judicious eyes. I doubt that any judge could have been more meticulous about inspecting the products: examining the jars of fruit and jam for an errant bubble or anything that looked the least bit off-color or too full or not quite full enough. This careful processing was just Mom's way, but she ratcheted it up a notch or two at fair time.

Our sewing projects could be fairly elaborate. We would start out by deciding what we wanted to sew for ourselves. Mom somehow managed to get hold of pattern books, Simplicity and Butterick books, and we would pour through pages of patterns for dresses and blouses. If we came upon a dress with a skirt that appealed, we knew we could get the dress pattern and make the bottom half into a separate skirt since it seemed like a waste of money to buy patterns for skirts only. Mom was clever and handy at innovating with patterns, so we counted on her to help us when the time came. Skirts were not that complicated, but blouses could be a challenge. There were collars of all different styles with different names—a round Peter Pan, an upright mandarin enclosing the neck, and regular pointed ones like a man's shirt; short sleeves and long sleeves that had to be attached to the main body of the blouse; seams all over the place where anything needed to be attached to anything else—the back side to the front, the collar to the neck, the sleeves to the armholes. In Mom's book, all these seams needed to be finished off, which meant they couldn't be left to fray with wearing, washing, and ironing. What a tedious extra step, adding that special stitch around the edges of the seams, but these details were likely to be some of the things the judges at the fair also inspected.

My sisters and I came home from the fairs with all blue and red ribbons, which meant all first and second places. In my imperfect memory, our blues outnumbered our reds, and we never came home with a white ribbon for third place. We would have felt humiliated coming home with a third after all the detailed, painstaking work that had gone into the cooking and sewing. Mom never said anything, but she probably felt some disappointment and puzzlement over the red ribbons. I don't think she could have figured out any more ways of being meticulous than she had already demonstrated.

Some girls, mostly girls from the ranches, skipped the domestic projects and went straight to showing their livestock. Showing livestock was a big part of every fair and was typically a boys' project, but there were no rules excluding girls. The most commonly shown animals were calves, steers, lambs, and sheep. I vaguely remember that pigs could also be shown but rather than being led around, they were kept in pens and the judge would walk through the area and inspect the various pigpens. I have no idea what the judge was looking for, but that was the only way a pig could be inspected since they were too unruly and un-trainable to be led around like a cow or sheep.

But showing a calf or steer was something to be proud of, the end result of a season of careful work: choosing an animal when it was a young calf to feed, groom, and get close to in order to parade him before not only the judges but also possible buyers. To be perfectly clear, these animals, all of them, were being raised to sell. What buyers saw in them was future tender steaks. A younger girl might show a calf—think veal—but I seem to remember that only girls who had at least reached adolescence would choose to show a steer. A steer could be a huge animal, the size of a bull, only castrated early on to direct the growth toward that tender and tasty beef, not toward reproduction. Calves, though smaller, were sometimes a little friskier, slightly harder to keep in line for the judges. Still, their size made a difference in the handling. While the calves tended to still look cute, the steers took on a majestic bearing. The girls were every bit as serious and competent as the boys in showing their animals. They would lead their animal before the judges and buyers maintaining full control: keeping it still; making sure the head, feet, and overall stance were correct for judging; being able to make the animal move as directed should a judge ask for that. The air would be tense with hopeful anticipation as the judges circled around each animal looking for flaws or added bonus points. A good showing, a blue ribbon, or especially a grand champion steer would not only make the girl proud but would usually mean a buyer was waiting in the wings.

My sisters and I never thought to show a calf or a steer since our family didn't raise cows for beef. We did have a few milk cows, and in my opinion they are the biggest nuisance of all to have around. The farmer can't take an extended vacation unless he can afford to have a helper (or a crew of helpers) on hand to take over all the daily chores, especially the milking. Dairy cows must be milked every single day at regular times, both in the morning and the evening. Their udders fill up regardless of whether you are there to relieve them. Even leaving for a day is a big deal, since someone has to be there to do the milking for that day and take care of the milk afterward. On our modest farm we had no more than two dairy cows at any given time, which sometimes made it feel even more onerous to have to be around for the milking. Just two cows; surely skipping an evening or a morning wouldn't matter. But alas, with dairy cows it doesn't work that way. We girls all learned how to milk, but my older sister, Lilian, was the one typically saddled with this chore. Although if asked, I could probably even now impress my city friends by showing off my milking skills—if they pleaded hard enough.

Though none of us ever showed a calf or a steer at the fair, one year my sister Mary decided she was going to show a lamb. We had been keeping orphan lambs in a large fenced-off area near the barn. I never knew the details, but Dad must have had an agreement with one of our neighbors who raised sheep. I say this not only because we ended up with the orphan lambs to raise and sell but because Dad helped this neighbor shear his sheep when the time came. I remember watching this happen. Each time, I would look on in wonder and delight as the piles of fluffy wool (our future skirts and sweaters) would keep getting bigger and bigger until one of the men would grab a pile and move it onto a truck or into a shed. The men doing the shearing were astonishingly quick: one minute there would be the sheep, looking big and round and fleecy, being forced to the ground and held there. A man with shears would immediately be upon it and move his shears rapidly over all parts of the sheep's body, the wool falling off around it as he moved. Just minutes later the sheep would be released, stand up in a daze, and shake himself a little before darting away. But what a transformation! A much smaller-looking, naked animal, almost shiny from being cropped so close to his skin. And not nearly as appealing as the fuzzy, fluffy animal of just minutes before. I couldn't help but feel sorry for the beast: manhandled, shorn of his Adonis locks, looking naked and homely, and probably shivering from the cold air he had never before noticed. I was thankful, both for the sheep and for us, that the wool was naturally regenerating. And to give credit where it's due, the man who shears the sheep, who rapidly and expertly moves his shears across the sheep's body without drawing blood or leaving too much wool behind, is a professional, a virtuoso, a pleasure and a wonder to watch.

The orphan lambs were not sheared; we never saw them grow to adulthood. Now I realize that they were sold early on to become the lamb chops that many of us relish bringing home from the supermarket. Nevertheless, we took care of them before that phase, and Mary was determined to raise one for the fair.

If sheep are stereotyped as docile and easily led, lambs must go through quite a transformation to become adults. Our little lambs were active and rambunctious and had ravenous appetites. Since they had no mothers to nurse them and were not ready for grazing on their own, we hand-fed them bottles of milk at least twice a day. The milk was cow's milk, and I have no idea what it might have done to the biology of a lamb, but it was probably nothing more than it did to us as small children drinking down glasses of milk. In other words, it nourished them with the nutrients they needed to grow and thrive. To my knowledge, none of the lambs took on unusual bovine characteristics from drinking cow's milk any more than any young human did.

At feeding time, we would take cleaned-up Pepsi bottles, fill them with fresh milk, top the bottle with a rubber nipple, and head for the farmyard. Like pet cats or dogs that suddenly materialize out of thin air when they hear their food being dispensed, the lambs would race over to the fence. It was a wire fence, the kind with large squares that allowed us to push the milk bottle through the square hole and hold it there while the lamb grabbed the nipple and sucked down the milk with astonishing speed, in a few minutes at most. In the process, there would be a lot of head and tail action from the lamb—pushing hard against the nipple and wagging the tail in spurts. We had to hold on tight to the bottles against all the bucking.

It was one of these home-grown orphan lambs that Mary decided to show at the next fair. After checking them all out, she made her choice, the one she thought was the best and healthiest-looking. She then became the one to feed it, talk to it, groom it, make it her own special animal. The lamb was coming along well, looking healthy, growing a nice coat of fleecy wool, becoming accustomed to Mary's voice and to having Mary around. And then, very suddenly, tragedy struck poor Mary and the lamb: the lamb fell ill, some animal illness that took its toll, making the unlucky little animal lose weight, become lethargic, and take on an overall unhealthy look. The lamb was sick, and there was no hiding it. I don't remember if it died or recovered, but the unhappy truth was that Mary didn't get to show a lamb that year. She was very disappointed, and we all tried to console her. But dwelling on the incident, carrying on about how sorry we were—well, that was not Mom's style or how any of us were raised. We all felt the disappointment and said so, encouraging Mary to think about next year, but then the subject was dropped. So after a few sorrowful tears, Mary also dropped the subject. That sabotaged attempt turned out to be the end for any of us trying to raise an animal to show at the fair. Perhaps there were other reasons that stopped us from trying again, but that is the one we all remember.

Raising anonymous animals for slaughter is one thing; raising an animal you get to know is something else. I know Mary would not consider doing that today, perhaps in part because she has lived in Denver ever since we moved there when she was in grade school. I think the adult Mary has lost all interest in raising an animal just so it could be slaughtered, but most kids who grow up on a ranch and remain there would gladly repeat the process—they keep hoping for a champion animal that will bring top dollar.

Having grown up on a farm, seeing animals live and die naturally as well as seeing them put to death for the pleasure of our palates, I think this kind of exposure can influence how we choose to eat as adults. But the direction in which that influence goes seems to be capricious. Some folks become staunch vegetarians. I never felt compelled to give up eating meat of any kind despite my experience around those four-footed creatures, petting them and handling them. I eat all kinds of meat except for the organs; I never took to the taste of liver. Perhaps my mother's style of cooking Japanese dishes that call for conservative amounts of meat and lots of vegetables influenced me more than anything and kept me from wanting to eat big steaks or large slices of roast at a single meal.

I was never happy to think of our calves and lambs being slaughtered for food, but on a farm, I accepted that that's what people did and that before modern technology, industrialization, and urbanization, that's how people survived. I knew that in our small farming community, that's what helped any number of us survive.

The Japanese have a reputation for eating lots of fish, and the Japanese in Japan are thought to be a healthy race because of this aspect of their diet. But for me, while eating meat is no problem, I have second thoughts every time I eat fish.

San Francisco used to have a large aquarium in Golden Gate Park. It has since been moved to Pier 39 and been redone completely. I have yet to explore the new aquarium, but in the old days when I was younger and had never seen any ocean life close up, never even seen the ocean until I was out of college, I would often go to view those beautiful and mysterious creatures, fish from waters all over the world. Walking slowly past each individual aquarium bay, looking at the fantastic shapes and colors of every kind of fish, watching as they darted past or slowly waved their tails and seemed almost to watch me watch them, I was mesmerized. I watched in a state of gratitude, for without a place like this, how else could I, could anyone, see these extraordinary creatures; how else could we get a sense of the abundance of life taking place below the waters that look to us standing on the shore so empty of anything alive? They were spectacular and for me, someone from the dry western Plains, unique. Even today, when I am in an aquarium and happen to remember that in some cultures fish are a main source of food, I momentarily experience a wave of nausea. I have learned to dismiss that thought as soon as it pops up.

Today, I will eat fish if it is the main course at a dinner party or if I'm with friends at a restaurant that serves only fish, but I never feel completely comfortable about it. Because try as I might, I can never erase the images from my mind—those graceful, colorful, fantastic shapes gliding through the water, stopping for a second to stare at me and look me straight in the eyes before gliding on to another corner of the aquarium. Fish should be seen and watched, not eaten.

If Mary's special project was her show lamb, mine was my insect collection, which I also entered for competition at the fair. I thought it was a very handsome collection, and I was proud of it. Why I chose to collect and show bugs, I no longer remember. It was an idea that came to my ten- or eleven-year-old mind. I didn't have a particular love for insects; nor did I hate them and want to destroy them. I think I wanted to do something different from showing an animal or homemade jams or skirts and blouses. Why not show bugs? Nobody else was doing that, and they were smaller than other animals, easier to handle, and not on the market for slaughter. It was also much cheaper to show insects than cows or sheep or pigs.

First, I went to the little library downtown. Even as a kid, I sometimes wondered how our very small town happened to have such a nice library. Now I know I have Andrew Carnegie to thank for it. It turns out that Mr. Carnegie was a staunch believer in free public libraries. He had come from an impoverished background and credited his visits to public libraries as the source of his education. He ultimately became an extremely successful businessman and industrialist, and with his massive wealth he established free public libraries all across the United States and around the world. Hardin had one of those libraries. Without Carnegie, I doubt whether we would have had a library, and my insect project would never have gotten off the ground. Today, when I think about it, I am truly grateful that I could go to my local, small-town library and check out several books on insects and how to identify them.

The next step was to find out how to kill them and prepare them so they could be displayed. I had to research everything, since the only thing I knew about bugs is that for the most part, everyone wanted to get rid of them wherever they were and that when they showed up on your floor or in your sink or somewhere else in your house, the way to kill them was to stomp on them and squash them into a dark spot on the floor. I would have to find a new technique, a way to snuff out their lives that would preserve their appearance so they could be displayed.

The way to show an insect, I read, is to pierce it with a very slender pin and stick the pin in some kind of case. The way to kill it without smashing it to death is to smother it with toxic fumes. The equipment needed was a "killing jar," special pins used solely for pinning insects, cigar boxes for displaying them, and cellophane for covering the cigar box "case." Not a project heavy on equipment.

Armed with my killing jar—a Mason jar with a perforated lid and a layer of absorbent rubber soaked in carbon tetrachloride in the bottom, covered over with cardboard—I was on the prowl for insects. At first it seemed like everything I encountered was prosaic, boring, not worth the effort of catching, killing, and mounting. Who would want to look at some bug we'd been stomping on at first sight for as long as we'd been alive? And that was certainly part of the effort: catching the old familiar bugs every farm family knew about and either ignored or destroyed. There were regular black beetles, the sweet little ladybugs every child plays with, some potato beetles that most farmers knew on sight. But I was happy to discover that there were also other, slightly more unusual types crawling and flying around, though one had to keep an eye out for them and be ready to catch them without damaging them in the process. Butterflies and moths were also part of my collection, and I found a few good ones. I don't have any memory of how I caught them without pulling the wings off. Their wings, I learned, were covered with a layer of pollen-like dust that would rub off on your fingers when you grabbed them. I had to be very careful how I handled them, how I opened and spread out the wings so they could be displayed without any smudges from my fingers. There was the ubiquitous pale yellow-green cabbage moth; a similar-sized butterfly with wings that were a shiny light blue when they were open and dull gray when closed; the state butterfly, its blue-black wings edged with light cream, appropriately called the mourning cloak butterfly.

When some of the local farmers learned that I was collecting bugs for my 4-H project, they occasionally saved me something they found that they thought was unusual. Once I received a letter in the mail from someone's mother whom I barely knew. Puzzled, I opened it and out fell a dead beetle, one I had never seen before. The gift of someone thoughtful enough to want to help me along in my project.

Watching an insect die in the killing jar was typically no big deal. The toxic fumes usually put them out very quickly, and I was able then to pin the bug and stick it in one of my cigar boxes for display. But the one insect I will never forget watching in its death throes was the grasshopper. At first, it would hop around frantically in the jar and spit a brown-colored liquid I called tobacco juice against the sides of the jar, those huge eyes staring out at me the entire time. After several seconds of this agony—or so it seemed—it would give a last feeble hop and flop over dead. I don't think I needed more than one or possibly two grasshoppers to display, but that scene remains vivid in my mind. While I can't remember what the other bugs did before they died, I don't think it was that dramatic.

To prepare insects for showing, I had to pin them and mount them and label them correctly for display. A true insect has six legs and three body parts: the head, the thorax, and the abdomen. Anything that looked like a bug but lacked that anatomy was not truly an "insect," so technically, I learned, a spider did not qualify—and they weren't amenable to being pinned either. The pin went through the bug's thorax, and I then stuck the pinned bug in a cigar box. When the box was full, I labeled each bug on the floor of the box and then covered the top with cellophane. I remember seeing Latin names in the insect books, but I used the common English names. I doubt that the end product was at all exotic. Most of the insects were ones that were found all around the farms in the area.

I don't remember much about my final collection, the insects I ended up showing at the fair. I don't even remember how many boxes I ended up with. But I do remember feeling pretty good about the collection and the effort it took to catch the little critters. It was a whole new way of seeing and thinking about bugs, for me anyway. So I was crestfallen that I took only a red ribbon, second place, at the fair. It was the only time I felt disappointed with my ribbon. I never said so in public, but I secretly felt I should have received a blue ribbon—A for effort—since I believe I was the only person of any age showing an insect collection.

Since that long-ago time, I have viewed a few professional insect collections in museums, and, of course, they are perfect looking: each insect is in mint condition, close to its natural color, legs intact, wings without any ragged edges or smudges from a careless finger, labels in Latin and English. And some of the insects are from exotic, hard-to-reach, or little-known places and are truly showstoppers because of their size, strange shape, or a color or color combination that can accurately be called out of this world. For some Americans, Montana may seem like it's out of this world—at least, it's hardly a well-known part of the United States—but its insects turned out to be pretty standard six-legged creatures, not nearly as exotic as those found in, say, Mississippi or Louisiana, states with closer to tropical climates at least part of the year.

When we left the farm, we left 4-H and fairs and competing for blue ribbons for good, and I have not missed the lifestyle. Even under the best of circumstances, I cannot imagine wanting to return to that life. I even lack the desire to raise a potted garden on the premises of my urban dwelling. I gratefully welcome any gift of fresh tomatoes or eggplants or zucchini from the bounty of friends who love to garden, but I have to find other ways to return the favor. And I definitely no longer have an interest in insects. While I don't need to stomp them into oblivion, my main interest, like most people's, is to keep them away from me.

Despite my early life or maybe because of it—those years of being around the primal beginnings of the food we enjoy—my preference remains to shop for the end product. That cut of meat on the Styrofoam tray covered with Saran Wrap, those unrecognizable kernels of corn transformed into corn flakes, those commercially frozen green beans that taste pretty much like green beans. But as I said at the beginning of this story, I am lucky enough to live in Berkeley, where food and everything about it is tantamount to a religion. If I want a pick-me-up, a shot in the arm, a break from the blues, one sure place that helps me is the Berkeley farmers' market.

The first time I went to it, I nearly burst into tears. It was gorgeous! The abundance alone was enough to make me cry. Booths and booths of vendors, around fifty of them, with their bounty beautifully displayed under white canvas tent tops lining both sides of a long block. They were selling what seemed like every vegetable and fruit known to humanity, and depending on the season, there might also be an entire booth of fresh-cut flowers in glowing reds, yellows, and oranges, with a few blues and purples thrown in.

There is always such an overwhelming abundance at the market that it is hard to notice that many things are seasonal. In the summer there are booths of stone fruit—yellow and white peaches and nectarines with their blushes of red or pink against the yellow of their skins; bright-apricot apricots; slightly later in the season, pears in greens, pale yellows, and bright yellows. Every fruit seems to appear in more than one variety, which means different shapes and sizes and levels of sweetness or tartness, firmness or softness. Earlier in the season there are fresh blueberries, which, to my deep regret, have a very short growing season. Fresh strawberries seem to have a longer season; and big, ripe, red juicy ones can be seen from spring almost through fall. Citrus—lemons, limes, oranges, tangerines, grapefruit, and something called pomelos, which look similar to grapefruits—take turns appearing and disappearing throughout the cooler months.

Naming all the vegetables could end up being boring since it would be such a long list, including all the regulars like lettuce, tomatoes, and potatoes—but looking at them is anything but boring. Who knew there could be so many kinds of leaf lettuce and head lettuce, some with heads compact and round and layered, the kind we see in supermarkets; some with leaves so large and spread out they barely hold a shape; others in compact little oblong heads? Small baskets of tomatoes the size of cherries or grapes or single tomatoes the size of a small grapefruit and every size in between, colored bright yellow and multiple shades of red, mostly round but sometimes oblong. The same with potatoes, no longer just the common brownish ones but purple, white, gold, and reddish-brown and ranging in size from a baseball to a golf ball, in shapes that range from oblong to a very knobby circle.

Then there are the specialty veggies that show up only during their discreet seasons, at best lasting only a few weeks: fresh pea greens, baby bok choy and rabe, sugar snap peas. Corn on the cob also has a relatively short season. Artichokes are popular and plentiful but are grown mostly in the moist Central Coast, while avocados are seen for longer periods because they come from Southern California as well as from places around the Bay area.

At the Saturday market—Berkeley has several throughout the week—nearly everything is organic, and on Thursdays, only organic vendors have permission to sell. Despite being organic, everything—all the leafy greens, the fruits, and every type of vegetable—looks nearly perfect. There are few blemishes of any kind, no wormholes, rotting spots, or hefty dark bruises. How this is accomplished I do not know since sometimes I can't even get a pear back to my home without stabbing a hole in it. The one exception I can think of to all this unblemished perfection is the corn on the cob. More often than not, there will be a fat worm nesting somewhere, usually at the top inside the silk, crunching away on the sweet, fresh organic kernels. My first attempt at buying this corn found me checking out and putting back every cob I inspected until I finally got it: that's what happens to organic corn. I have watched in knowing amusement as many customers do the same thing until they, too, finally shrug their shoulders and toss the cob into their bag.

In addition to being organic and flawless, my favorite part of the farmers' market is that it doesn't matter what time of year I shop there; I always find fresh lettuce and other fresh veggies. The market is closed the week of Thanksgiving and the week between Christmas and New Year's—and that's it. A twelve-month farmers' market makes it seriously difficult for me to remember what month I'm in.

It takes me a long time to wander through the market. I don't buy that much, but I always look. I cruise along, checking out the produce, nibbling the samples as I encounter them—and there are lots, since along with the fresh produce there are stalls of locally grown nuts, dried fruit, hand-pressed local olive oil, bread, cookies, pasta, pastry, ice cream, and chocolate. Because the market is open through the lunch hour, some vendors sell lunch—tacos and burritos, Thai and Indian food, and some vegan dishes. My usual last stop as I head for my car is for the chocolate chewy, a flourless cookie—you're given a discount if you buy more than one. Hard to resist a bargain.

After growing up in Montana where the growing season for fresh food lasts about a minute in comparison to what I have just described, all I can say is this: we Californians are completely spoiled by our year-long bounty and completely clueless when it comes to how the rest of the country must think about, grow, and shop for food. Thank goodness we in the Bay area have made composting an artform, since we probably have more to compost than some areas have fresh produce to eat.

I confess, I stopped going to church some years ago, but if I want a religious experience, I take myself to the farmers' market.

Sometimes I chide myself for not taking more of an interest in growing at least a little of the food I eat. Many of my friends and acquaintances grow something they can eat and share with friends, and they've always done so, even when they were young and just starting out on their adult journeys. Sometimes it's just one vegetable in a big pot—maybe a tomato plant or an eggplant or a few little heads of leaf lettuce. Sometimes they rent space in a community garden where they can plant their own favorites to eat. Sometimes they have space enough in their backyards for raised beds where they grow a full array of edible plants, including medicinal herbs. As I mentioned before, I welcome their bounty with open arms whenever they bring me some, but I have less than zero interest in growing anything myself.

My lack of interest in—indeed, my lifelong resistance to—growing anything for myself makes me fear I will be seen as ungrateful for the farmers and farmworkers who toil to feed folks like myself. I fear they will think I don't get how hard they work and, most of all, how hard their work truly is. But it is exactly the opposite: I know firsthand, from personal experience, what it takes to be a successful farmer. Actually, I should modify that statement a bit since successful farmers on big farms in today's world now have a large amount of technology at their fingertips to assist them in every aspect of farming, from testing the soil to gathering in the harvest to predicting the weather. I have only witnessed this growing phenomenon discussed on television programs; I've never personally talked to a farmer about how technology has affected his or her farming techniques.

But all farming has a relentlessness that I still feel deep within my bones. Technology must still be operated and made to be useful, and plants and animals still need attention day in and day out. Farmers still cannot take off whenever the spirit moves them; when they do leave on vacation or for a break or an emergency, the plants and animals and sometimes the machinery must still somehow be attended to.

Back in the 1960s when a generation of young people—most of them urban hippies—were talking about "going back to the land," building little cabins, becoming self-sufficient by growing their own food, I could never get onboard. On a good day, I wanted to warn them that it was not as easy as they might think. When I was feeling more cynical, I wanted to laugh at them and say: "You have no idea what you're talking about or what you'd be getting into. You have never been eye to eye with a cow, let alone milked it, or had to plow a field or harvest a crop bigger than a flowerbed in your backyard. You can't stop work to toke up anytime the spirit moves you, and you can't just leave because you want to hit the road for a few days or weeks or because you're sick of working *every single day*. Farming is demanding, actually relentless work. Farming is not for the faint of heart or something to be done on a whim." My guess is that I didn't need to lose any sleep over these clueless hippies, these innocents, since the overwhelming majority of them never went on to try their hand at farming. And neither did I. I remember enough and have enough of the farm girl embedded in my cells and tissue that I have no illusions about living off the land, about going back to a "better" time, about being self-sufficient. Give me the city any day, the supermarket with all its prepackaged food. But especially give me a farmers' market where I can surround myself with the bounty of the land, revel in the pure beauty of it, and pay personal homage to the growers who brought their bounty to us. The colorful array of perfectly shaped, unblemished fruits and vegetables dazzles my eyes and fills my heart. I have learned over time not to be greedy and take more than I can use, but it's hard to be judicious as the impulse is to take a sampling of everything because it looks so tempting, so delicious—so sweet, so crunchy, so juicy, so fresh. I return home with my favorite choices of the day—and feel spiritually renewed.

I started out saying that I don't like to cook, and my hand-picked treasures from the farmers' market have never changed that. My lucky and spoiled default option has been to go, as often as my budget allows, to a Berkeley café or restaurant and have a superb meal made from the freshest, tastiest ingredients grown within a few miles of here and expertly cooked—all by someone other than myself.

10

Pictures on the Wall

I see their pictures wherever I look—in newspapers, on television, on the internet—so there is no need to add them to my file, already overflowing. My head is bursting with the images: men, women, children, families—bedraggled refugees, their sandaled feet scuffing up a small trail of dust behind them as they move quickly across the dry, unmarked terrain, through brush and scraggly trees, the hot sun overhead casting their short shadows in front of them. Their faces are etched with fear, fatigue, confusion; their eyes are glazed and empty or filled with panic; their arms are carrying babies, goats, household goods, or sometimes one arm balances a bundle atop the head—another way to transport their clothing, bedding, food. The younger and stronger wrap their arms around the shoulders and waists of the old, withered, and infirm or have small children strapped to their backs.

It seems that just last week, or was it yesterday, they were regular people, living regular lives. But complicated twists of an indifferent fate have dislodged them, uprooted them, made them refugees, sent them pouring across invisible borders, fleeing guns and bombs and missiles from land or air, tanks or armed men on horseback.

I look at their pictures and am filled with helpless anger and sorrow. (I can't help remembering those other painful pictures, pictures of Americans, Japanese Americans: the children stoic, with identification tags around their necks, their parents standing close, looking worried and confused . . . The elders, faces blank, sit on suitcases or the traditional cloth *furoshikis* packed full with bedding and clothes. They are guarded by soldiers with rifles. They wait tensely at a train station, but no one will tell them where they are going—or why.)

Some refugees pull behind them thin animals on tethers of rope—cattle or the ubiquitous goat. Sometimes they have had time enough to fill a cart with their belongings, and someone barely up to the task, either too old or much too young, pulls or pushes it along. I wonder, is this a blessing, to be able to get away with more of their possessions, or is it just a heavier impediment on their escape into the unknown? (I am remembering my parents and Lilian, forced from home on a moment's notice, taking with them only what they could carry . . . Only yesterday they were regular people with regular lives. Now they are homeless, uprooted by an unjust twist of fate.)

These everyday people are fleeing their homes in Sudan or Darfur or Congo or Mali or Libya or Syria or Iraq or Palestine or Afghanistan or Pakistan or Myanmar or Ukraine or not long ago in Bosnia or Albania or Chechnya or Guatemala or Chile or Honduras or El Salvador or Cuba or Nicaragua or Haiti or Vietnam or China or Tibet or Lebanon or Iran or Zimbabwe. I'm sure I've missed some places. Not all of them are fleeing manmade instruments of destruction. Sometimes it's floods or earthquakes or other natural disasters. I think of Louisiana or New Jersey or Oklahoma right here at home. (I am remembering the coasts of Washington, Oregon, and California after Pearl Harbor was bombed . . .)

Occasionally, a TV newscaster will give a number to these fleeing masses, and it is almost beyond belief—hundreds of thousands, millions—and there appears to be no letup. All of them are on the move; all of them want to survive. And the price for survival is high. When refugees leave their state or country, they also leave a common tongue used to share a story, a rumor, a secret, a joke; they leave their farms in the countryside where they consulted the night sky to learn when to plant and harvest their crops. (I am thinking of those Japanese American farmers who worked the rich farmlands of California's central valley, growing produce for the rest of the country; or tending the orchards of Oregon, lush with ripening fruit snatched away from them at the peak of its ripeness . . .)

Some refugees are fleeing familiar villages and towns where they once had thriving shops or cafés or roadside stands. (I'm remembering the shops and markets and cafés of Little Tokyos or Japantowns of Seattle, San Francisco, Los Angeles—successful businesses vacated but not emptied of possessions, also ripe for the taking . . .)

And now the scenes rise up swiftly, some of them conjured out of the gaps in my family's stories, some of them remembered moments from my own past, long held in silence:

My parents in Seattle, among the many listening for news, hearing rumors, and wondering. "Do you think they will send us away?" "I heard we might go to jail." "Maybe they will shoot us—that's what I heard." "Nothing! They will do nothing of the sort! We are American citizens. Don't talk crazy."

Their apartment in Seattle in the moments after they left it for the last time. What happened, I wonder, to what was left behind: the couch and chairs; the dishes, pots, and pans; the beds and bedding; and especially all those treasures—knickknacks, pictures, vases—objects no one else would understand or find meaningful?

Those American concentration camps, the ones their friends arrived at, in the hot, sandy deserts of Arizona, California, and Colorado; the heavy, humid swamplands of Arkansas; the high, dry mountain plains of Utah and Wyoming. I once went with some students on a pilgrimage to Camp Amache in the Colorado desert, long after the war ended. I have lived in the high, dry heat of the mountains and have felt the oven-like effect the sun has on the body. The searing heat of this flat desert land felt even worse. I couldn't imagine working outside, planting trees and making gardens in this unrelenting heat, but we saw the evidence of such labor: the trees, planted by the incarcerees and still standing by the rim of the foundations, had grown tall after thirty or more years.

My dad, still young, arriving in his old hometown as a refugee, cautiously optimistic that he could find work. He had graduated from high school there; some of the local sports enthusiasts knew of him. He was on the short side but had a solid build and was versatile; he had been quite good at football, a team sport, and boxing, which honed him individually. But after his arrival in

Sheridan, making the rounds of people he knew and thought would give him work, his optimism took a swift kick in the gut. No one would hire him, and they gave him that tired, unconvincing excuse: it was "for his own protection."

The fields of sugar beets, one of the main crops on our new farm, the rows seeming to stretch for miles under the Montana skies, the deep-green beet tops, river water glinting in the irrigation ditches. When Dad found himself roundly rejected by the people in Sheridan, he'd jumped at the chance to start his own farm. Montana was the place where the land was, land the US government was leasing to grow sugar beets to help alleviate the cravings of the sugar-starved populace the world over.

Another Japanese American farmer, not my father, years later, in another state. It was the early 1980s in San Francisco, and he was testifying to the Commission on Wartime Relocation and Internment of Civilians, a federal commission investigating the forced removal and incarceration of Japanese Americans. I can still clearly hear his thin, barely audible voice as he explained that in the year of the forced removal, he had had a bountiful crop of "beautiful ripe strawberries." He was proud of the way they had turned out, large and red and sweet. One day, near harvest time, government officials showed up out of nowhere and, without asking, confiscated all of it. The farmer hesitated and his voice cracked a little when he talked about his beautiful red berries. The dead silence in the room when he finished speaking seemed like a tribute to his lost berries.

Our farmhouse, too small for our family of six. The outside rundown and the inside not much better. Everything about it reflected how our lives had been put back together in bits and pieces, in a hurry. The living room sofa that revealed little patches of white created in a former life by repeated rubbing from various body parts. A set of used kitchen chairs that needed new seats.

The kitchen table, the center of our home, more like the center of the universe because it was round and that's where our family life happened. I have no idea where it came from, it was just always there. It was solid oak, a sturdy table that could withstand whatever four children, their parents, and any visitors might chance to assault it with. Everything of import, from quiet conversation to rambunctious children doing projects or acting out, happened around that table because it was big enough and strong enough to handle it. I liked looking at the beautiful color of the grain running across the top, but I rarely got to see it because Mom kept it covered with a bright, patterned oilcloth tablecloth—the kind every farmer's family used at that time—to protect it. I don't know what happened to it after we moved to Denver, but I suspect the sheer weight of it convinced Dad that he had to leave our beloved table behind.

The bookcases in our farmhouse, remnants and reminders of city life. The first was narrow, with maybe four or five shelves filled with different kinds of books. I can only remember a few of them, oddly not so much the titles but the authors—books by Isak Dinesen, Ernie Pyle, John Hersey (we had *Hiroshima*, his book about "the bomb"); the Grimm and Andersen fairy tales; Alice in *Wonderland* and *Through the Looking Glass*, classic children's tales. A hot Montana summer afternoon might find us sisters leafing through the Alice books since they had pictures and most of the others didn't. On the weightier side, we had a full set of the *Encyclopedia Britannica*, not found in every farmhouse circa 1949, shelved alphabetically in the larger glassed-in bookcase. On one of those shelves were two art portfolios of standard-page size, kept closed with little ties. They contained reproductions of classic paintings: Mrs. West, a beautiful dark-haired woman with hooded eyes; a bare-breasted Liberty leading soldiers in a charge (I couldn't understand why she had a bare breast—why wouldn't she take a moment to cover herself?); the portrait of George Washington with the unfinished, cloudy white bottom; other pictures I don't remember. I don't know why none of them were ever framed and put on a wall. They just remained in their boxes, treated as though they were precious originals.

Dad's old college notebooks, discovered by my sisters and me one afternoon in the farmhouse. They were filled with drawings of mechanical things we didn't recognize. But what fascinated us even more, as we sat squinched together poring over every page, was how meticulous and exacting—how perfect—every line in every drawing was. Thinking of them now, it was as if they had been done by one of today's computer programs. It was hard to believe our dad, with his thick, rough farmer's hands always doing hard farmer's labor, had made these precise, delicate drawings. As we continued to look through his notebooks, we found other pictures: trees and landscapes, artistic sketches done in pencil. Even though I was just a kid in grade school, I felt the mismatch. I felt like I had discovered that underneath his khaki shirt and dusty work jeans, my dad was really an artist—so what was he doing on a farm?

• • •

Dad was a man of many talents, with interests that ranged from art and music to machines and what made them tick. But the exclusion marooned him on the farm, and as he plowed his fields, he must have watched his dreams go under along with the Montana soil.

No one can say that Dad didn't give farming his best try, but in the end it got the best of him. His hired field hands were mostly young men, and they would come and go as the spirit moved them—sometimes to land of their own, sometimes to romance and family life. So he was usually left to manage on his own. Over time, the financial ledgers became more and more unbalanced, the red ink far outweighing the black, so when Mom and Dad announced to us kids that we would be quitting the farm and moving to Denver, I can't say I saw it coming, but I also wasn't surprised.

So there they were again, Mom and Dad packing up to move, this time with three of us girls helping out, trying to keep our little brother out from underfoot. Then off we went to set up yet another home. For my parents, this would mean moving from city to country and back again in just over a dozen years. In mobile America, many people make many more moves in that stretch of time. But for my family it was not just the moving: it was that their forced removal from Seattle had driven them out of the city and home of their choice and initiated their lives as refugees searching for a place to land, looking for a place to call home.

It wasn't easy at first, moving from the isolation of our farm to life in a city surrounded by buildings and people—overwhelmingly white people—and everywhere lights, noise, movement. While I would never have guessed it at the time, those books and pictures and magazines of Dad's had opened our eyes and minds to so many things we hadn't seen around us on the farm; they served to lessen the shock of adjustment and helped pave the way to life in the big, white, urban world.

I am not sure whether my parents really loved Denver or whether they were just sick of making big moves and starting over, but we stayed there, and both of them are buried there. When it was my turn, as a young adult just out of college, to think about where to live, I was eager to move on. As a family, we had never had the finances to take vacations or go anywhere exciting, so I was ready for some adventures far from where I had spent most of my young life. I had nothing against my parents or my parents' home; I was just impatient to explore the world around me and beyond. I took for granted that someday I would have a home and a family, but that was just a speck way off in the distant future. Right now, I told myself, I had places to go, things to see.

It probably turned out to be a good thing that my parents weren't able to fund my desire to wander and explore the country or the world. They weren't able to bail me out if I got into trouble. It was on me to pay my own way, whether that was in the pursuit of a job somewhere across the country or of an opportunity to do something I felt drawn to, however capricious it might seem to my parents. This responsibility gave me the freedom to explore the world in my own way. Which was to keep on the move.

It never occurred to me that I should stay in one place and settle down. I didn't think about putting down roots, going deep into life instead of going broad. Moving didn't seem like a big deal to me—in fact, I seemed almost allergic to staying put. After all, I had been through moves with my parents, and now I had friends who had moved away from their family homes when they went to college. We, all of us, were starting to look for jobs, getting ready to embark on the next phase of our tender, budding lives. A number of my new friends were from California and wanted to return there, especially to the Bay area, because it was the mid-1960s, and the Bay area was a place that gave pretty much uncensored permission to the youthful experimentations of the time. Not wanting to be left out, I followed my friends. We told ourselves we were out to change the world, and we believed it. So we jumped onboard the already crowded hip and colorful renaissance train of the 1960s as it rolled headlong into San Francisco.

My friends seemed to take to it like ducks to water, and I watched as they found jobs that set them on the path to careers they believed in. They found apartments just right for their needs, and they made time to eat, drink, party, and dance to the psychedelic "vibes" and music of the 1960s with old friends and new ones. Over time, they began to make long-term commitments to boyfriends or girlfriends—they were actually giving up living "in sin" and getting officially married and talking about having children. We all seemed to have started out driving VW Bugs and having no trouble moving our entire lives in those cars, but those days seemed to be fading away—my friends' cars morphed into bigger models, their apartments had more rooms, and their debts began to accumulate with the purchase of houses and the bigger cars.

I seemed to be the holdout. Although I loved the unparalleled diversity and the mad, creative energy of the Bay area and I loved my friends, I couldn't help but feel like I was missing something. There was something out there that I wanted, so I kept searching, kept moving around. In the early 1970s I ended up back in Denver and took a job in Boulder at my alma mater, the University of Colorado.

From there, taking my cue from the universe, I decided to go to grad school and chose the one that was farthest away, the one that was 2,000 miles from my present location in Colorado and on the opposite end of the country from California. The one in Boston.

I found Boston fascinating, so different from anywhere else I had lived. And I loved being near so many other interesting East Coast cities, all easy to get to by train. I made friends and was stimulated and challenged by the intellectual atmosphere. I fell in love with the autumn foliage, the colors even more vivid and gorgeous than any pictures of them I had seen. I made somber and curious explorations of the old graveyard a few blocks from my apartment. And I never tired of listening to that strange Boston accent where vowels and consonants were left out and added to words in what seemed to be a completely random fashion, leaving the sentence still somehow comprehensible. But when I graduated after two years in Boston, I thought nothing of moving cross-country again in search of a perfect job.

Even with my newly minted psychotherapy degree, I was finding it hard to penetrate the protected walls of academia to find another job, so when I was offered a position counseling parents and families at a preschool modeled after Head Start, I happily accepted. It wasn't the exact job I was looking for, but the tradeoff was that it was in San Francisco, and I had to admit that I was missing California and the Bay area. I was actually feeling as though I could settle down someplace in the East Bay—though it was a feeling I didn't fully trust. But I was determined to stay beyond my two-year limit in any given place, to shoot for at least five years before making any major geographic changes. One unintended benefit of this decision was that I had met a man I really liked and now had time to nurture a relationship with him. He was a Bay-area convert committed to living there, and I felt committed to him. I could feel my roots grow deeper when we decided we were ready to move in together.

"Wait! Wait a minute! Stop! What are you doing?" Me, in a state of alarm.

"I thought I'd hang this picture on this big, empty wall. It needs something, and this is a great piece of art. A friend gave it to me. It could easily be in a museum." Him, with earnest enthusiasm.

"What? You call that *art*? *Museum-quality art*? Looks to me like it was made by some acidhead who thought painting when he was stoned would make him an artist. No way! That's not going up on *my* living room wall."

We were in our first apartment together in Oakland, having a serious fight over what to hang on a vacant living room wall aching for decoration. His choice was an original picture he'd been given. I had been willing to consider some of my family photos. After my sarcastic, stubborn putdown, it was a full twelve months before anything filled that wall.

Finally, one day my partner came home with a large matted print of a Gauguin, one of those pictures of bare-breasted native women surrounded by lush greenery. The size was right and the colors gave the room new energy and cheerfulness. I helped him hang it without further "discussion."

But the truth was that I liked that wide expanse of blank whiteness. I was not in the habit of ever hanging anything on my apartment walls. I was not unaware of this quirk, this resistance to decorating the walls of my living quarters. But from my earliest days I had never put any pictures on the walls, not even of family, something most of my friends did out of respect for theirs. In fact, furnishing a new place was never a big interest of mine. It didn't appeal to me to shop for grownup furniture like couches and matching chairs or matching place settings of dishes or silverware.

On one occasion in the late 1960s, in my early days of living in Berkeley, I went to Telegraph Avenue with a girlfriend to look for household furnishings for her new place. At the time, Fraser's, now long gone from Telegraph, carried stylish, higher-end merchandise for homes: dishware, fancy decorative vases and glassware, some furniture. My friend would pick up something, a piece of hand-blown, sculptured glass, and coo, "Oh, look at this! Wouldn't this look great in my living room? Really spiff it up. Take away that Woolworth look I'm trying to get rid of."

"Oh yes, very tasteful. Go for it," I'd say (thinking, and please hurry so we can get our cappuccinos at the Med). She was right; the piece was all she said it was, but I could care less. It had nothing to do with me. I made do with a few un-chipped plates (to keep my mother happy, since that was her bottom line—no chipped anything on her table); a few pieces of silverware, enough to have a limited number of friends for dinner; a bed, sheets, and a few warm blankets; a pot big enough to boil spaghetti; a frying pan, a saucepan, a tea-kettle. At some point down the road, my sister sent me a rice cooker. Most of what I had in my early adult life was stuff I could easily pack up and take off with.

Now here I was, more than a decade later, trying to set up a decent household with my future husband and his young daughter who stayed with us part of the time. I knew that was what people did when they married and had families: they strove to make a home; they strove to establish a feeling of stability and permanence. I wanted to make this happen for these two people whom I loved, but I was not convinced that I could actually do it.

I had never before thought to ask myself: What makes a home? I wasn't sure I understood what a home really was. Looking at home furnishing magazines wasn't all that helpful; even I knew a home was more than a house with fancy furniture and tiles of granite or marble (if you could afford them) in bathrooms and kitchens. Surely there was somewhere else, somewhere besides a magazine I could turn to. As an English major who had always found poetry abstruse and frustrating, I was surprised when it was a poem that helped me work it out.

In his poem "The Death of the Hired Man," Robert Frost has the farmer, Warren, and his wife, Mary, discuss this question of home. Mary tells Warren that their former hired man, looking tired and unwell, has returned home to their farm to die. Warren, not as sympathetic as Mary, reminds her that the man is undependable and walked out on them when they needed him most. Warren mocks Mary's use of "home" and gives her his definition: "Home is the place where, when you have to go there, / they have to take you in." Mary simply says: "I should have called it / something you somehow haven't to deserve."

Warren's definition still jars me, sending me back to those ubiquitous images of fleeing refugees, both in this country and globally. They have crossed borders into a neighboring country or state or county willing to take them in. A "home" for now. But often, as the newcomers' numbers swell, the hosts can no longer accommodate those streaming over their borders, taking refuge in their villages and in their homes. The demand for food, clothing, and shelter outstrips the supply. Thus some of the new arrivals are forced to move on again, making yet another destination their "home." I now remember that this is what happened to the Japanese Americans when they were evacuated from the West Coast. Many thousands of them were forcibly removed from their chosen homes and made to live in the awful barracks-style buildings thrown up for them in the harshest locations in the country. Those barracks would be "home" for three years or more—until they were closed and the next journey began, either back to a place that had changed in their absence or on to a new destination, a new start. A few thousand others, like my family, were dispersed around the country, making places like Chicago, Cleveland, Utah, Wyoming, and Montana "home" for who knows how long.

But I realized, in that Oakland home, that it was Mary's definition that gnawed at me, that had brought me back once again to this particular poem: "something you somehow haven't to deserve." Did I deserve a home? From my transient lifestyle, it could be read that I didn't think I did. So far, I hadn't allowed myself to slow down long enough to ask the question and search for an honest answer. But I knew that my time for this kind of moving around was running out. I knew it was time to settle down if I was going to make the necessary home for the family I was starting to build. I knew it was time for me to take an honest look inward and ask myself what was holding me back. The mere thought of this overwhelmed me and left me feeling limp as a rag doll, but at least I was able to stop my impulse to follow my usual pattern: ignore what my body was feeling and just keep moving on. So for once I made myself stop, take a deep breath, and see what poked its way into my consciousness. Rather than finding curiosity and restlessness, characteristics I liked to flatter myself that I had, I was only a little surprised to find that it was fear. In my past, whenever I had felt a twinge of fear, I quickly ignored it and acted like it didn't matter; what mattered was not to let on to anyone else how I was feeling, to act perfectly natural and forge ahead.

But now that I could name the demon, I had to ask the other glaring question: What was I afraid of? This time, what came up shocked me because it seemed so obvious: What was the point of putting all that energy—financing, furnishing, decorating—into something I would end up losing sometime down the road? Why bother? My fear, buried beneath my conscious awareness, conveyed to me that my home would be snatched right out from under me, not because I hadn't paid my rent or my mortgage or been somehow irresponsible—I was always meticulous about those things. That was the scariest part of all: my home would be snatched away through no fault of my own. Some unforeseen, shadowy, shapeless force would sneak up on me and take away any home I fixed up, furnished, decorated, poured my heart into, made my own. It would strike like lightning—quick, unpredictable, destructive. I didn't know when, and I wouldn't see it coming until it was too late for me to act. My only option was to outsmart the home-snatcher by keeping at least one step ahead of it—not stay in one place too long, not acquire anything precious or valuable to lose in the first place. I would have no pictures to remove from walls, no boxes of dishes or silverware to pack, no furniture or collector's items to fuss over. I could be gone in a flash.

Without realizing it, I had become my parents, reenacting the drama of their exclusion with every move I made. When they were forced to leave their Seattle apartment so many years before, they had had no say in the matter, no choice as to whether they could stay or go. It was an order from out of the blue, coming from the very top—the president of the United States. They *had* to go and go right away; it was just a question of where. There was no time for my mother to mourn over all they had to leave behind: all the small treasures people had given them, all the things they had worked so hard to acquire on their own. Whatever my father was feeling, he never let on; he pushed himself forward without flinching.

So, ignorant of my unconscious need to relive my parents' legacy, I had kept on the move—city to city, sometimes state to state, or from one apartment to another. Each time I had moved, I'd believed I was making a perfectly logical, reasonable decision. I'd believed I was making a conscious choice based on some practicality, like finding a job or going to grad school. I didn't get that the person I called "I" was not the one making the decisions.

Of course, I had no control over being born in Wyoming and moving to Montana shortly afterward or moving to Colorado in my adolescence. But on my own in adulthood, there were Illinois, New York, Pennsylvania, Massachusetts, Washington, DC, and California. I had told myself that I was seeking the perfect job—that elusive combination of service and a paycheck I could live on, the one that fit my moral values and standards. But now it was dawning on me that there was much more to my restlessness than I had suspected.

Perhaps one reason why it took me so long to grasp the meaning of my prolonged transient lifestyle was that I didn't remember ever feeling like anything but the outsider, always the new kid on the block. A transient lifestyle could momentarily enhance that feeling, but it was nothing new. When my family left our Montana farm, we left the one community of Japanese American friends we would ever have, however far apart our farms were. In Denver we had my mother's big family to relate to, but it turned out to be rare for everyone to get together in one big group unless it was a special occasion. We knew there were districts in Denver where most of the Japanese Americans had settled during and after the war years, but we ended up living in an all-white neighborhood and going to all-white schools because Dad wanted us to get the best education available. When we learned that the Japanese American community gathered in two main places in Denver—Simpson Methodist Church and the Denver Buddhist Temple—we could hear the bat slice the air as we took our third strike: we were Episcopalians. But hardest of all was having to tell other people, mostly other Japanese Americans, that honestly, my family had never gone to an incarceration camp. It was a story few of them were familiar with, and it made further conversation awkward. If we hadn't shared the hardships of camp life, if we hadn't shared the comradeship, if we hadn't stuck together to help each other survive, then what did we have in common?

Perhaps not much. Growing up in a white world, surrounded by white people, I knew that just about everywhere I went I would stick out, be noticed, because I looked different. I felt like an oddity.

As a child, I knew that at home we ate different food from everyone else—not much meat, lots of rice, veggies, and tofu—even if we kids loved burgers and French fries just like all the other kids at school. I knew that while my parents always spoke English to us kids, they spoke Japanese when they were around my grandmother and some of my aunts and uncles and sometimes when they wanted to share something private between themselves. I knew that at school I was making headway with the Copernicus axiom, learning to act as though I considered myself the center of the universe, at least in the classroom. Thank goodness I had two sisters I could talk to about these subtleties since they were having similar experiences at school and since, besides them, there was nowhere for me to turn to get a reassuring reflection of myself.

With time, careful observation, practice, and the ongoing demand to fit in, I eventually adjusted, not only because I had to but also because I wanted to. I wanted to fit in and have a life, a life as much like the lives of everyone else as was possible. So on the surface, I seemed to be no different from my friends. At school we belonged to the same clubs, ate the same food, laughed at the same jokes, and enjoyed the bits of gossip floating around the halls and schoolyard. I did the best I could to dress like them and interact the way they did when it came to socializing outside the classroom. But part of me knew all this was superficial because underneath, the barriers of race and especially my parents' income imbued me with a deep fear that someday I would be "found out."

After college and leaving my parents' home for good, in those years when I was fleeing from the home-snatcher, I had made California my default home. Time and again after trying out one place or another for one reason or another, I had returned to San Francisco and the East Bay. I returned after graduate school, after a brief job in central New York, after the breakup of a relationship. Early on I had made friends here, people I considered kindred spirits; each time I returned to the area, we picked up our conversations pretty much where they had left off, sometimes years before. And now it looked like I was making my own family here. The stars seemed to align: work, friends, romance. What more could I ask for?

After a lifetime of feeling uncomfortably conspicuous, perhaps the strongest draw, the one that made me feel most "at home" in the Bay area, was the way it *didn't* feel. At first it felt strange *not* to draw second looks or sideways glances; *not* to feel as though I stood out like a blinking neon light; *not* to feel like a social curiosity; *not* to leave people wondering how they should react to me. The Bay area of the late 1960s, the 1970s and into the 1980s was peopled both by folks who looked like me and by lots of others who didn't: dark, light, and every shade in between; short, tall, large, slight; some foreign, some recent immigrants, many old-time residents. No one seemed bothered by seeing groups of young children who were a chaos of shades from dark to light playing together on a playground or in a yard; no one seemed to look twice at couples on the sidewalk, hand in hand, one dark, the other fair, or both some shade of dark but with features nothing like one another, whose ancestors had perhaps lived thousands of miles apart. It was non-news. And it was non-news for me to show up to a party at someone's house and find that I was not the only person who was not white. For me initially, it was a surprise; then it was a huge relief. This geography of hills and sea and harbor, this fantastic mix of people, all were offering me a home, the kind of home I'd never had before. It felt like a gift from the universe. I should seize the opportunity.

Time, without question, pulls down on our muscles and leaves them in places we know they don't belong. It causes us to give a second glance in a store window before we recognize our own reflections. But when I take a backward glance through the time of my life, I recognize and am grateful for those moments of luck that shaped it.

And there have been lots of those moments. Even growing up poor in America, I had many material advantages not found in most other parts of the world where the poor often don't survive and the ones who make it do so in spite of their surroundings. My family had a house—nothing fancy, very basic, but occupied only by us and not shared with a flock of relatives, friends, or strangers. I went to free public schools and received what proved to be a decent education. My parents believed that all their children should go to college. I assumed that I would go when the time came, and I did. I had the chance to choose a profession and a career and engage in meaningful work. And while there were times growing up when I didn't feel this way, I now am grateful that I had to come to terms with being physically and culturally different from mainstream America. The experience of learning to comfortably navigate in two different worlds has allowed me to enter some of the other cultural worlds that exist in this country. I have met people and made friends who have privileged me with a glimpse into their communities, and by doing this they have made my world bigger, more complex, less capricious, and less dangerous. I am not saying that when the world opens up to you and you to it, it gets more logical, but it does start to make a lot more sense.

With age, exposure, and the wisdom gained from living life, I find myself standing closer to those friends who insist that all of us, wherever we may be on the planet, regardless of what we think or believe about the world, are connected to each other in a web-like fashion. It's akin to a law of physics.

Here is my bad news—and good news: it has become much more expensive and much more work for me to move because now I do have those boxes of dishes and kitchenware, those chairs and a couch and a table and some pictures that I treasure, either purchased or given to me as gifts. I have fulfilled the maxim that space allowed is space filled.

Still, I can't seem to shake the images of those benighted refugees. Sometimes when I close my eyes, their fugitive bodies rise before me. The children especially haunt me. I know some of the puzzling questions they will have to wrestle with on their way to adulthood. Who they are and where they belong will be for them more than passing adolescent existential questions. And sadly, many will continue to feel that they are perpetual outsiders, no matter where they are or how long they have been there.

Tragically, many of these homeless children, some of them orphaned, won't survive to adulthood. But for those who do survive, I know that finding a permanent shelter may not be enough to make them feel safe and secure. If I could, I would tell them "you will know you are home when you can hang pictures on your walls."

Epilogue

Bananas and Beyond

Back in the late 1960s and early 1970s, back in the days of Black power and Yellow power and La Raza and Red power, when people of color were loudly, proudly claiming their ethnicity by naming their color, back then I happily embraced all of it—but I was always a little bit afraid. Afraid I would be revealed as a fraud: I would be discovered as never having had a community of other Asian Americans, as having grown up in predominantly white communities pretty much my entire life. This fear wasn't completely unfounded. In communities of color, there were often hierarchies of how one was viewed, and somewhere toward the bottom were "oreos" for Blacks and "bananas" for Asians: folks who were black or yellow on the outside but white on the inside. I was scared I would be considered a banana.

Not to be misleading: I didn't come from a lineage of bananas. Neither Mom nor Dad was a banana; nor was either one plagued with invisible self-loathing. Mom's Japanese behavior as she had learned it from her parents was never something she tried to cover up. She cooked and we ate Japanese food on a regular basis—in fact, at almost every evening meal, even after we moved to the city. She spoke Japanese to her elders and to anyone who preferred it over English. And she made us kids tow the line when it came to respecting and not talking back to our elders, sacred tenets of polite Japanese society.

With Dad, I have spoken about his intelligence and his many skills, including drawing and playing the piano. He could also speak Japanese and was able to read it passably. These characteristics made him widely respected in our Japanese American farming community in Montana. Mr. K, who was one of the most successful and wealthiest members of the group, was especially fond of Dad and admired his intelligence and his ability to get along with just about anybody. As I think about this now, I also think he admired Dad for his quiet but effective demeanor, so opposite from his own ebullient social style.

Dad also made some interesting decisions about his family and about being among white people. Perhaps Dad was a pragmatist, or maybe he just observed accurately and had strong powers of analysis. He could tell by paying attention who made it in society and how they did it. Or possibly he just figured out what he had to do to help his children make it in the white world, especially to help us get the tools and skills we needed to avoid replaying his own experience of trauma and loss, humiliation and disappointment as a result of powerful and sweeping racism. We had to know who we were dealing with, inside and out. We had to navigate the white world with confidence and intelligence and fortitude. We had to be able to fight fire with fire.

That was one reason why, when we moved from the farm to Denver, Dad found us housing in an all-white neighborhood where we went to all-white schools and made nearly all white friends. Mostly, I never thought anything about this, since living in a nearly all-white world had pretty much been the experience of us kids all along—the major exception being those early years in Montana when we lived on the farm near other Japanese American farmers. As young children, we interacted with them and their kids socially whenever we had the chance. But even then, when we started school, our schools were mostly white. Our few Japanese American peers ended up going to a different small rural schoolhouse closer to their farms.

So by the time we started school in Denver, while I was not unaware that I was Japanese and that all my peers as well as my friends were white, I didn't feel like a complete outsider, like an alien from another planet. I'd been here before. I knew there were white social behaviors that were very different from what I had learned in my Japanese family, but like Dad, I too, had learned to pay attention, and as I went along I picked up the social nuances of the white world. One of the most dramatic and alien expectations was that I, like everyone else, would speak up and be noticed and heard without being asked my opinion or what I was thinking or needing at the time. I understood without being told that if I held back, I could be judged as dumb or unprepared for class. I did the best I could at this formidable task, but even today, as an aging adult, I still experience a slight adrenaline rush when doing this.

My student years in the Denver schools I attended were years when I felt accepted, and I can honestly say that I don't remember ever experiencing overt or covert racial prejudice from my peers. If there was any from my teachers or the administration, it wasn't the kind that was so obvious that even a young student could see it or feel it. I am now convinced that this was the case because my singular presence never posed a threat to anyone. The school was white, I was not; I was the one who needed to be aware of those around me. As most people do, I reflected back what I was seeing—the behaviors, language, clothing styles, hairstyles of my peer group. I grew to be comfortable at my all-white school, and I made some good all-white friends. It wasn't until much later in life—during the tumult of the 1960s and the war in Vietnam, when identity politics erupted onto the social conscience—that I started to wonder: Was I a banana?

Fortunately, I was able to grasp the language, rhetoric, and social analysis of the movement that was capturing the young people—especially the college students—of the time and to understand the issues. I could analyze the movement's message and see how it did or didn't apply to me and my life—starting with the way my parents' experience diverged from that of the vast majority of Japanese Americans of their generation. I knew that my parents had suffered the singular experience of the group of American-born citizens who were forcibly removed from their homes along the West Coast just because their ancestry was Japanese. I knew that they had lost everything in that moment, including their right as citizens to protest or resist in any meaningful way. I knew that nearly all those who had been forced from their homes had been imprisoned in American concentration camps, most of them for up to three years, until the end of the war. I also knew that the forced removal was why my family had ended up as poor, struggling farmers in Montana.

And I knew that because of our unusual separation from the larger group, the forced removal had affected the lives of my siblings and me in ways that were markedly different from our peer group of Japanese Americans. My parents had become separated from the Japanese Americans who, after the war, left the concentration camps and returned to rebuild their urban communities in the cities along the West Coast, restoring as best they could their old lives as professionals, as gardeners, as students, as common working folks trying to make an honest living. My parents had been relegated to a farm, and farming was a complete way of life. One doesn't just wake up one morning and walk away from a farm. So the decided downside of not being forced into a camp was that when the war was over, my parents were unable to rejoin their friends and return to Seattle to pick up the pieces of their former urban life. In other words, my parents no longer had a community to relate to, one that could support them as they, in turn, supported the stability and growth of that community. Though their struggle had been so different from that of their peers, I knew my parents had endured as much as any other Japanese Americans at that time, and I knew they had paid their dues. Sometimes I allowed myself to imagine what our lives might have looked like if Executive Order 9066 had never been issued—my father being able to complete his degree and become a professional, my mother remaining connected with her circle of women friends, my siblings and I growing up in an intact, thriving Japanese American community—and I felt full of rage and sorrow.

I was not in the mood to forgive and forget my own government's racist sins. I knew this would not help anyone in the future who wanted to stand up for justice, equality, freedom, and all the other rights Americans so proudly claim we exemplify. No, I was definitely not a banana. But I wasn't sure what others saw when they looked at me, before they got to know me.

I have talked about my unsuccessful attempts to find and fit into my Japanese American peer group at the University of Colorado, the place where I first began to consciously explore my Asian American identity. And my adult quest to fit in continued for decades following those college years, with little better luck or results. I have finally had to admit that my life growing up surrounded by the white world left me bereft of a Japanese American—or any Asian American—community that I could take for granted as my own. Whenever I was around a group of Japanese Americans of my own age or any age, I always got the feeling that people were checking me out like they would anyone and couldn't quite figure out what to make of me. Not that anyone was rude, but it was transparently clear that I was an outsider, and not just because I hadn't been born in the area or didn't grow up around J-Town. No, I was an outsider in a more fundamental way that showed up in how I talked, laughed, related to others, looked or didn't look at people I was with, all the subtle nuances that make up culture. The phrase "my people" wasn't one I could use with honesty beyond referring to my own family of origin. Yet to a passerby, I looked like one of the crowd.

The best I could come up with to describe myself is that I was a hybrid, defined by the Oxford Dictionary as something that is the result of combining two different elements. I like this description better than "banana" since it encompasses the fact that my parents never let me off the hook from behaving like a polite Japanese youngster and then as a proper adult woman when I was at home or in the company of other Japanese people. I knew the social rules and ignored them at my peril since I was always my parents' daughter and not a completely separate individual. But I also could navigate the white world without fear of being excluded because I understood how to behave among polite white company. I may have been considered a little reticent and "quiet" by my white peers and their parents, but I knew it was considered normal to speak up, be heard, be noticed, and have an opinion to stand behind. That wasn't always easy or comfortable for me to do, but it was something I understood as completely acceptable, even necessary, so it was the behavior I aimed for in white company.

I have clearly stated that I didn't and don't regret the way I grew up, even though it has meant that I haven't had my ethnic community to fall back on and to automatically provide me with a place of comfort and a sense of security. Once or twice I heard my mother say that the forced removal of Japanese Americans turned out to be a good thing since it forced them out of their comfortable all-Japanese communities and scattered them around, forcing them to intermingle with whites and other types of people. I was pretty young when I heard her say these words, but even then she didn't sound convinced or convincing. Maybe she was trying to justify her own losses and her life of separation and isolation. However, what she said turned out to be true in my life. Since I have never lived in a comfortable Japanese American community, I've been continually challenged, for reasons of both chance and choice, to branch out into a world different from my own. Now, looking back, I am grateful that I was challenged.

My Denver junior and senior high schools were located in a well-off residential area of the city. Both schools were big and served a large population of middle- and upper-middle-class white kids. I grew up hearing about families going on vacations, about parents and older siblings traveling abroad, about my classmates' dance, piano, violin, and other types of lessons—all indications of culture and financial ease. It was everyday talk, and the travel stories always made me feel a little envious. They fed right into my own desire and fantasies about traveling the world, which I had had ever since we lived on the farm.

So it gives me pleasure and pause to say that whatever else has or hasn't happened in my life, whatever I have done or not done that was on my to-do list as a young adult, I have managed to do some traveling. The pause part has to do with all there is left to see in this big world. The truth remains that even though I feel I have seen a few places on the planet, there is much more that I have not seen and still long to see. This jolt of reality in any sense of overblown sense of self-accomplishment I might have been harboring was rudely brought to my attention when, yes, I was on a much-anticipated trip. I was at a game lodge in South Africa, and after coming back from a drive in the bush viewing animals in their natural habitat, I spoke to one of the other tourists, an American woman who was there with her husband and two daughters, one a teen and the other a year or two younger. A white family, polite and slightly abrupt. I told her how impressed I was with the way her daughters seemed completely at ease on the game drives and weren't ruffled when a large elephant had approached our jeep and hovered her trunk over the head of one of the girls. The girl had remained perfectly still and composed. The mother responded, "Oh yes, they've traveled a lot. They've been on five continents." That stopped me short since I'd never heard anyone speak of their travels in terms of continents. It had never occurred to me to keep count—of continents. So feeling not the least bit competitive, I immediately tallied up my count. Hmmmm. Only four. Clearly, if I wanted to keep up, I had more places to go, things to see . . .

But humor, storytelling, and false competition aside, when I think of my family and my two sisters, I think of how we all talked about traveling when we were growing up on the farm and in Denver. We all wanted to see the world, and we all ended up taking at least a few good trips outside the United States. My brother did it differently, traveling to Japan and living there for nearly a decade. My surviving sister continues to travel, as do I. Their children have also traveled outside the continental United States. They are young adults and will undoubtedly continue to explore.

I realize that traveling abroad is something middle-class Americans have always done and have talked and written about for decades, so I am not talking about anything astonishingly new and different here. But what I am saying is that for my family members and myself, traveling has been its own particular symbol, proof that somehow we weren't so different from our white friends and their families, that what we wanted and valued in life was not that different from what they wanted and valued. We traveled in spite of the fact that money has always been tight and that others didn't expect it of us. Our parents could never afford to fund such activities, so we waited until we were working and had jobs and could take vacations whenever and wherever our pocketbooks would let us. Our high school and college friends may have been given trips to Europe for graduation, but I was thirty and had finished graduate school before I went to Europe for the first time. My sisters likewise were well out of college when they first traveled there. Even after we had jobs and had to work every day to earn our livings, our curiosity about exploring the world never waned.

From what I can tell, our Japanese American counterparts, the ones we didn't really have a chance to rub shoulders with, have not, as a group, been avid travelers. I think this has been changing over time, especially with the fourth and younger generations. But when my siblings and I were traveling, we were still the exceptions. We didn't mind. We were having a great time.

I can own my personal sense of what gives me wanderlust. I have talked about it in other stories, but what is important for me to say again is this: that not having had the security of hailing from a Japanese American neighborhood, of not getting to know myself by seeing my reflection in my peers and my community, of having to question on a regular basis who I was in terms of behaviors and tastes and how to relate to and interact with people, all that has ended up being a blessing in disguise. Of course, there were times when I felt alienated, isolated, frustrated, and sometimes depressed. Times when I felt challenged on so many fundamental levels. But the way I was forced and, later, forced myself to be open to differences of every kind—to notice them, to question them, to accept them or not—shaped my interactions with the world at large and made me realize that the only way forward was to be as tolerant and accepting as possible, to try for kindness and looking after one another. These goals are only ever partially realized within me at any given time, and I know they will never be fully achieved and are, in truth, impossible to sustain as a constant state of being. I try not to let that realization keep me from persisting.

I wouldn't recommend that a young person seek out growing up as the only one of their kind in their schools, neighborhoods, and communities in general. But I do know that being the "only one" also opens up opportunities: chances to take on what is on that tray in front of them, to get out of their comfort zone, to go on a trip, to check out another place—a city, a state, another country, or another neighborhood on the other side of town. From my experience, something new and different, a "foreign" adventure to plumb and explore, can only help you in the long run to interact and indeed cope with a world that is changing—and shrinking—at breakneck speed and will continue to change faster than most of us could ever have imagined. It seems now more than ever before that we all need ways of keeping our minds and our hearts open and willing.

A while back I promised my sister Mary that I would send her our father's college diploma so she could look at it, hold it, and experience the wonder of its improbable journey into existence and into our hands. But it still sits on my desk where I can see its blue cover. I think I am reluctant to relinquish it just yet. Probably because it's one of those symbols that encompasses the core of my family's story, of my story.

As I've made clear elsewhere in these stories, my parents, especially Dad, were fanatical about education: all of their children were going to get a college degree, that was a given. And that fact was ever more immutable because of Dad's experience of having the chance for his own college education rudely, shamefully yanked out from under him. I am glad that both he and my mother lived to see all four of their children grow up and become college-educated adults. We all went on to careers, and we all were successful in that we were able to use our professional training to maintain our independent lifestyles.

When I think about how my siblings and I all made traveling a part of our lifestyles, I believe we saw it as an extension of education, not that it would give us anything concrete beyond a few pictures to show. But all of us knew there was a world out there waiting for us to discover. And this reality was only reinforced by our interactions with our white friends and the white urban world we lived in. Travel was commonplace in their lives.

What I don't think was clear to me until I had the experience of collecting my father's diploma is that, speaking only for myself, my travels were not done just out of curiosity and a deep desire to see more of the world than my own immediate environment. My desire to travel also came from a need to finish something for my parents, for my dad. That unrealized college degree, that education interrupted, that profession that never materialized—those were the things that hampered and obstructed my parents' ability to see and explore the world on their own. After removal to Wyoming and Montana, their struggle was first and foremost to survive. It was left to us, their children, to do the things they had wanted to do but couldn't because their lives had been so suddenly derailed and stripped of choice and resources.

I realize that on the surface, this story of parents sacrificing their own youthful dreams and desires in the service of raising their children is not unusual. But it is my hope that the stories in this book, the stories of my life, reveal how my parents' lives tell a tale beyond the norm of hardworking immigrant families and their hardworking, successful children who become proud, mainstream Americans. My father's university diploma, his college degree conferred on him well after his death and tragically unbeknownst to him, stands for that other immigrant story—of how even second-generation American-born citizens can have their most cherished hopes, dreams, desires, futures cruelly stolen from them by the highest powers of the land, never to be recovered or returned to them in original form. Thankfully for all Americans, the story doesn't end on that disgraceful and disreputable note. As I have tried to show, my parents went on to have decent lives and raised their children to have the "better lives than theirs" that most parents say they wish for their children. And I again express thanks to the University of Washington for honoring my father and the others who were thwarted in their journey toward higher education. Seeing, touching, actually holding my father's diploma contributed a powerful, almost mystical inspiration to tell my parents' story.

Perhaps the greatest lesson I learned in making this journey, in trying to follow the frequently obscured path of my parents' lives, was that it was incumbent upon me to be consciously grateful to them for their selflessness and their sacrifices and for making it possible for me to live my own life. A life I have tried to live with as much integrity, compassion, perseverance, and, ultimately, as much humility as they lived their lives. Even if I fall short, it is the most honest tribute I can think of to honor George and Rose, my parents.

Afterword

Lane Ryo Hirabayashi

Many are familiar with the fact that over 110,000 persons of Japanese ancestry, almost 70,000 of whom were US citizens, were subject to incarceration in American-style concentration camps during World War II. It is not as commonly known that for three months in early 1942, the federal government encouraged Nikkei (people of Japanese descent) to move east of the military zones that had been set up in California, Oregon, and the state of Washington. This move, which the government called "voluntary migration" (US Department of War 1943), is worth considering here because it provides the historical context for Judy Kawamoto's *Forced Out: A Nikkei Woman's Search for a Home in America.*

To begin with, "voluntary migration," along with "voluntary evacuation" and "voluntary resettlement," is one of a number of euphemisms that wind up disguising the fundamentally repressive nature of this move. As a result, these euphemisms suggest that those who chose to leave the West Coast before the end of March 1942 were different from the Nikkei whom the United States Army initially rounded up and then confined. This is an assumption, however, that *Forced Out* forces us to question.

What does the extant literature tell us about Japanese Americans' so-called voluntary migration in 1942? After Pearl Harbor and the US entry into World War II, Nikkei became increasingly anxious about the hostility toward Japan, an animus unfairly projected on Japanese Americans especially in the West Coast states where ethnic settlements in some urban and rural settings made Japanese Americans quite visible. Suffice it to note here that although there were thousands of Japanese Americans in California—the densest ethnic concentration in the lower forty-eight states—Nikkei never constituted more than 2 percent of that state's total population before the war.

As local, state, and national pressure against Japanese Americans began to build, military leaders in the Western Defense Command conspired with the Provost Marshall General's office to round up and confine the West Coast Nikkei in a supposed effort to contain any possible threat to national security (CWRIC 1983).

Even though cognizant that the building climate of hostility might lead to incarceration, Nikkei who were willing to head east had very limited time to pack up their belongings and move outside of West Coast military zones. Given all of the logistics involved in making the move, however, and the often hostile reception along the way as well as in their point of destination, approximately 5,000 persons did so—a relatively small cohort, all things considered (Niiya 1993).

Readers should keep in mind that *Forced Out* is not necessarily a typical account. Rather, Judy Kawamoto's narrative offers us a series of fascinating, albeit complex, vignettes about the personal impact of fleeing the West Coast in early 1942. Kawamoto's bent toward reflexivity, in combination with her professional training in psychology, makes her especially adept at self-analysis. In this sense, Kawamoto is able and willing to share a wider range of thoughts and feelings than most Nikkei of her age/generation would typically articulate. Moreover, *Forced Out* is one of the first personal narratives along these lines that spans a lifetime, recounting a Japanese American woman's reflections on her youth, adolescence, college, professional, and retirement years.

At the same time, Kawamoto's account is deceptively complex because she references herself during at least four different life stages, from a child to a mature adult. This, in turn, raises thorny methodological issues: When we hear Kawamoto's voice, who is actually speaking? For example, is she accurately and fully recounting her thoughts as a young girl? Or are we listening the whole time to a mature adult who selectively remembers her emotions and thoughts during childhood, allowing us to glimpse parts of her subjective memories, albeit filtered through her hindsight as an adult? Thus, while appearing to be nonfiction, *Forced Out*, like all biographical accounts, poses tantalizing questions having to do with what Kawamoto does and doesn't remember and will or won't say, as well as how to factor in subtle nuances such as how the passage of time and the course of her postwar biography have impacted her narrative.[1]

In the end, Kawamoto's narrative indicates that any hard-and-fast contrast between Nikkei who were confined in American-style concentration camps and those who moved east before Executive Order 9066 was carried out may be overdrawn. Both populations—those who were forcibly confined and those who were forced east—were *compelled* to move as a result of external factors beyond their control, uprooting them from their homes, lives, daily routines, and support networks.

Beyond these disruptions, the displacement was life-changing and traumatic for both families and individuals. For the first-generation Issei, mass removal and incarceration was more of the same, only worse—the culmination of decades of prejudice and discrimination that made them unwelcome aliens in a country where naturalized citizenship was not an option because of their race (Daniels 1962). To the extent that the public educational system was a key socializing factor for the second-generation Nisei, they understood themselves to be citizens of the United States and therefore entitled to the benefits and protections guaranteed by the US Constitution (Yoo 2000). In short, each of the key generations in pre-war America—Issei, Nisei—was traumatized; for many, anything that had to do with Japan—whether language, religion, culture, identity, cuisine—had to be eschewed or at least hidden if they were going to be able to rise above the hatred and suspicion the war generated (Nagata, Kim, and Wu 2015).

---

1   It is significant that published depictions of the experiences of Japanese American "voluntary migrants" tend to appear in the form of fiction. One example (Kawaguchi 2007) seems to draw from family biography but was in fact published as a novel. For experiential accounts, nothing beats the Densho Project's online oral histories (densho.org /category/oral-history/), some of them featuring detailed narratives having to do with the so-called voluntary migration. Although given by interviewees decades after the fact, these accounts are still an invaluable resource for anyone wanting to understand this dimension of the Japanese American experience during the 1940s,

As a result of these processes, the lines of cultural transmission and continuity were often and sometimes severely disrupted. For Nisei and the older Sansei who survived the 1940s, this meant that family history could be fragmented by elisions and even outright silences in regard to a wide range of critically important information. As a result, so much of the literature of Japanese America after the war has to do with an ongoing, if not endless, process of claiming, reclaiming, and sometimes inventing family and personal narratives in an attempt to fill in the lacunae. That is unfortunate, to be sure. Still, it is in the telling of personal stories, such as the account Kawamoto bravely shares with us, that there is hope for healing as subsequent generations try their best to measure the impact of "the great betrayal" on their kith and kin (Nagata, Kim, and Nguyen 2019).

In sum, it is clear that moving east and thus avoiding removal and confinement was not the end of her story. Rather, as Judy Kawamoto so powerfully expresses, it was the beginning of a lifelong search for identity, meaning, and ultimately home that her 1940s displacement engendered.

References

Commission on Wartime Relocation and Internment of Civilians (CWRIC). 1983. *Personal Justice Denied*. Washington, DC: US Government Printing Office.

Daniels, Roger. 1962. *The Politics of Prejudice: The Anti-Japanese Movement in California and the Struggle for Japanese Exclusion*. Berkeley: University of California Press.

Kawaguchi, Sanae. 2007. *A Time of Innocence*. Bloomington, IN: Xlibris.

Nagata, Donna K., Jackie H.J. Kim, and Teresa U. Nguyen. 2019. "Processing Cultural Trauma: Intergenerational Effects of the Japanese American Incarceration." *Social Issues* 71 (2): 356–370.

Nagata, Donna K., Jackie H.J. Kim, and Kaidi Wu. 2015. "The Japanese American Wartime Incarceration: Examining the Scope of Racial Trauma." *American Psychologist* 74 (1): 36–48.

Niiya, Brian. 1993. "Voluntary Migration." In *Japanese American History: An A-to-Z Reference from 1868 to the Present*, edited by Brian Niiya. Los Angeles: Japanese America National Museum.

US Department of War. 1943. *Final Report: Japanese Evacuation from the West Coast, 1942*. Washington, DC: US Government Printing Office.

Yoo, David K. 2000. *Growing Up Nisei: Race, Generation, and Culture among Japanese Americans of California, 1924–1949*. Champaign: University of Illinois Press.